SCENES FROM THE PAST : 26 (PART FIVE)

JOURNEYS BY EXCURSION TRAIN FROM EAST LANCASHIRE

KIRKHAM TO POULTON,
BLACKPOOL (NORTH)
and FLEETWOOD
for the ISLE OF MAN

COMPILED and WRITTEN by STUART TAYLOR

(Above) The beautiful ornate and elegant brickwork of Blackpool North station is seen above. It was a real Victorian treasure. Our family visits in the 1950's and early 1960's to this station were very limited until the closure of the Central station at Blackpool took place in 1964. Having walked along Topping street and up Talbot road this is the view that would greet us each Friday on the last day of our excursion week of rail outings. As always we would be making our way to Fleetwood for the market. **(right)** Ronnie Hilton who hailed from Leeds was a real star in those heady years of the 1950's. The haunting strains of *'No Other Love'*, his 1956 hit record still send a shiver through me. It really was the big summer hit that year. He could still be heard at Blackpool right through the 1960s.

COPYRIGHT © STUART TAYLOR 2005
ISBN 1 801197 74 6
ALL RIGHTS RESERVED
DESIGNED BY STUART TAYLOR
PUBLISHED BY FOXLINE (PUBLICATIONS) LIMITED
P O BOX 84, BREDBURY. SK6 3YD
PRINTED BY THE AMADEUS PRESS,
CLECKHEATON, WEST YORKSHIRE

Other Foxline titles by Stuart Taylor

To Blackpool for the 'lights'. Possibly the best remembered steam happening ever at Blackpool took place on Saturday 30th September 1961. As the cold air signalled an end to the summer season and the nights drew in, and the illuminations excursion trains coasted into Blackpool in a steady procession, two very special trains took the north line that day. The Northern Rubber Company's annual outing organised by Alan Pegler brought 60022 *Mallard* from Retford via the Calder Valley and Copy Pit, to Preston and on to Blackpool. Rose Grove's Rennie Lonsdale took over the driving seat at Sowerby Bridge through to Blackpool, (see rear cover). **(Above)** Here we see the first of those two very special trains that reached Blackpool that September Saturday in 1961. Approaching Kirkham and running along the Down Fast line at Dowbridge are the restored Midland Compound No. **1000** and **45548** *Lytham St. Annes*. It is about 12.25 (dinner time) as 1T07 from Stoke Golding passes by, the train included two sleeping cars. Soon, 1X08 from Retford with the gleaming *Mallard* will pass the same spot. There was an atmospheric end to the day as just before midnight, the return excursion for Retford eased out of Blackpool North into the cold night air with 60022 *Mallard* the train engine being piloted by the compound No. 1000. *Paul Claxton*

09920499

Poulton No. 3 signal box. (above) The No. 3 box was all important at Poulton. It regulated trains trains travelling to and from Blackpool and Fleetwood and protected the entrance to the station as well as routing trains via the avoiding lines (the Up and Down Fast lines), those which skirted round the station from the No. 3 signalbox to No. 1 cabin heading out towards Singleton. The lines curving away to the right are those leading to Poulton No. 5 and Thornton on the line to Burn Naze and Fleetwood.

Contents

From the box. Looking out of the signal box window at Kirkham South Junction, we see Lostock Hall's **45421** getting under way and making for Preston after calling at Kirkham in the summer of 1965. Bob Jackson looks very much like the fireman who is attempting to blot out the landscape here. Over to the left, new housing now occupies the old internment camp down by the station. The fast lines over on the right would come out of use in 1965 and would be steadily rusting during 1966 before being lifted by Preston ballast turns during the summer of 1967 and removed in sections to Kirkham goods yard. We will go into more detail about that in the final volume which highlights all the events of those not so swinging sixties. *Paul Claxton*

Dedication. This book is dedicated to Fleetwood engineman Ken Bradshaw. Whenever I've driven a train to Blackpool or indeed thought about the railway to Fleetwood, Ken has always been there with me. His words of wisdom and knowledge of railway working generously imparted, just never leave you. **(Above)** The 'Lizzies' were amongst Ken's favourite engines. When it came to leaving Euston, and keeping the smoke down, Ken was a true master in firebox management.

Acknowledgments: Roy Anderson, Barry Atkinson, Ken Bradshaw, Josephine A. Brady, Tony Bretherton, Archie Buchanan, Paul Claxton, Jack Cookson, Ken Davis, Dougie Dunstan, Peter Fitton, Alan Gilbert, Bert Holland, Michelle J. Howe, Steve Leyland, Jim Markland, Brian Pickersgill, Don Rutter, Chris Spring, Peter Walton. *Lighthouse Stationary* at Fleetwood, Helen at *Colne Copy Shop*, Supervisors and Staff at Blackpool North (*First North Western and Network Rail*). The Foreman and Fitting Staff at Blackpool North Carriage Sidings and Depot (Enfield Road); Family assistance with computer work is appreciated. Thanks to Barbara for the use of her computer; to Robert and Gemma for guidance; to Richard for artwork and picture restoration. Sincere thanks to former footplateman Derek Eastwood for his encouragement and getting me back 'on track' with 'physical therapy' back on the 'steamers' - it did a power of good. Finally a special thank you to David Blore of York for restoring my life.

Thank you one and all
Stuart Taylor

Introduction

Well, here we are at last, the book everyone seems to be waiting for and which is fast becoming known simply by the term 'twenty six - part five'. It's been a while as they say and I do seriously regret the delays. Personal circumstances in the last few years have turned my life inside out, leaving me at times with little will to continue doing anything. To have attempted to finish the book as events unfolded just would not have worked. I'm extremely grateful for your continued interest and kind words about my books, thank you one and all. This book was designed to be the last in the series and would cover not only Blackpool North and Fleetwood but would take us through the Beeching years of the middle 1960s to the end of the steam era. As the superb later years material began to come in, it quickly became clear that there were too many brilliant large for-mat pictures to cram into one volume. Also, the story that I want to tell of just what happened when Beeching's boys created the sale of the century and took away most of the railways to seasonal seaside resorts like Blackpool, Morecambe and Southport, had considerably expanded. Add to this the fact I was always going to do a reprise, looking back at how the books evolved and show the resorts we visited in quick fashion as an update to the 1964 period. In this way, you can see there was a whole book on its own, just about those years of change. So there will be another (final) volume, Twenty Six - Part Six, or if you like, number twenty six (the final chapter).

In this volume, the journey begins at Kirkham and takes us to Poulton and Blackpool North. There we will see the 'stars' of the 1950's in a section looking at the show business side of seasonal life through to 1962. Changes in the entertainment world came very fast by 1963 as again we will show in the reprise edition. Then it is off back to North station to begin our journey out to Fleetwood, but not before visiting the North engine shed as it was in the 1950's and up to 1962. Here too, we will revisit the shed in the reprise volume to come, showing it in those run down years of 1965-67, when diesels often outnumbered the steamers and the excursions as a whole were far fewer in number. There you have it, there is a lot to look forward to and a good read, as they say, in this book. If you knew North station and the railway to Fleetwood, then this book is full of the atmosphere of the period of the war years, the early 1950's and the start of the 1960's. If you enjoy the read, let me know via the publisher, I will be most grateful.

Stuart Taylor
Colne 2005.

Kirkham South Junction. On Saturday 21st May 1961, K3 **61922** rolls into Kirkham with excursion No. N925 from Wakefield. Picture by *Paul Claxton.*

5

BLACKPOOL ENGINEMAN DON RUTTER

Don Rutter and Dougie Dunstan. They were always the best of mates, even years after Don left railway service and Dougie transferred to Crewe. Don, seen above on the right, poses with Doug outside Don's home in the early 1960's at Westmorland Avenue in Blackpool. In helping me prepare these excursion books on Blackpool, Don was a gold mine of information despite having left the railway behind when Blackpool Central closed in 1964. He'd kept track of where the men from the shed at Rigby Road had got to in the intervening years. He was also very good at recalling events and placing people who appeared in pictures. Dougie moved from Blackpool to take a position at Crewe where he still lives today. The ten years that Don spent on the railway ensured his memory was not clouded by changing railway events of the last thirty odd years. What he recalled was just as clear and crisp as when it happened. Whenever I visited 'Raylands', Don's home on the Marton for a natter, the welcome was always warm in railway fashion and the kettle wasn't far off the boil. We sadly lost Don as I began to put this book together in earnest. He had trotted round in his usual manner collecting things for me and visiting old mates to ensure I had every help possible in portraying the whole story of those excursion years. He was keen in his pictures to portray the human angle and I have always considered it a vital aspect of these books. When part four came out and I took him a copy, his face lit up and he said *'hee, fame at last'*. Taking a camera to work was never easy on the railway. Taking your 'mates' pictures at work, rather than the engines, or as well as, often helped. Don was readily aware the happy band of men at the Blackpool sheds were soon to be disbanded, so he set about recording the men and the work where possible and we are very grateful indeed that he did. Thanks for everything Don………

Rigby Road shed in 1960. (above) On the shed roads by the Kelbus sand drier are **45617** *Mauritius* of Carlisle's Upperby depot and **46165** *The Ranger (12th London Regiment)*, which was a Preston engine at the time. This was just the way Don would remember the shed roads at Rigby Road depot in those final years. He had trained big diesels like the English Electric Type 4's and it was clear they would soon be covering most of the express work with engines like this. The spectre of single manning was talked about and in just a few years time an agreement allowing many forms of train to operate with only a driver on board was accepted.

Don was keenly aware that the accountants were taking over the running of the nation's main transport system, their only wish being to make the books balance whatever the cost in terms of jobs and security. He therefore decided to capture the daily scene whilst he still had chance. As those last years of his footplate career unfolded, Don set about making a personal record of the people he had worked with so he could look back upon it in future years when the team of driver and fireman would be no more. Seen right and over on page 6 are two human interest views that Don was so good at. In 1960 when he was booked with top link driver Bill Davis, they rode back one day from Crewe 'on the cushions' and Don snapped Bill in the train as they passed Lea Lane bridge near Salwick, and then as they walked back up to the shed as Bill chatted with his brother who was on the Per.way. Don quickly took two pictures of them with the Central station as a background. An every day scene we all did, walking about the railway to and from sheds and the like, but something which is now quite priceless. ***Don Rutter***

FLEETWOOD ENGINEMAN - KEN BRADSHAW

Ken Bradshaw at Fleetwood station. This rarest of snaps is just a little contact print and it shows Ken on the footplate of **'5214'** at Fleetwood station just into B.R. days. His regular mate, driver Harry Wilkinson, took the picture just before they set off for Crewe from Fleetwood's No. 5 platform with a fifteen coach special boat train taking internees on their journey home. The picture is lucky to have survived all this time. It was carried around for years before Ken put away in the glass cupboard for safe keeping. There were a number of Black Fives shedded at Fleetwood over the years but 5212 and 5214 always seem well remembered. They both arrived on the Fylde around 1945/6 time from Low Moor shed at Bradford and thankfully the former engine mentioned is still with us. This engine 45212 also worked the last steam train into Blackpool South as the steam era ended in 1968. Both these locomotives were noted for being strong and free steaming.

Picture via *Ken Bradshaw*

I always said that if I ever did write a book about railways and it included Blackpool and Fleetwood, then I would dedicate it to engineman Ken Bradshaw. Looking back now over the years it seems that I was destined to meet and work with Ken, though it may quite easily have never happened at all, in which case I doubt very much if you would be reading this volume covering Fleetwood. The thing is that I came to know Ken years after our excursion trips ended, though there is every danger back in the earlier 1950's Ken may well have been on the engine which took us from the North station at Blackpool to Fleetwood. It is Ken's memories of his time at Fleetwood loco, together with my own recollections of the Friday outings to Fleetwood that has made the second half of this book possible. After the 'steamers' had finished and the railways locally were in a mess, the Colne – Skipton line had closed, making getting to work difficult. I left the railway behind and took a job in the mills locally. Soon redundant, I was just about to settle in as stores controller with Foulds lifts when a job came up at Glen View golf course in Burnley. Ken was the head greenkeeper there. Instantly, we had a lot in common despite the age difference. It had been something like fourteen years since Ken had himself left railway service and taken

a job weaving over in Nelson. He was quick to take up an offer to work on the local Golf course. The year I spent with Ken between 1972/73 passed very fast as each lunchtime in the barn messroom, we sat round the coke stove nattering about the railways locally and not so local. We discussed the LMS days and the war years when Ken was just into his early twenties. The places Ken talked of, I could instantly see in my mind just what he was describing, being uncannily real. The talks were full of atmosphere and even now years later I still sense it. You really did sense the war years, the era of George Formby, of dancing at the Winter Gardens and so on. It all seemed so alive. We talked of places he worked to and passed through, such as Preston, Chorley, Bolton to Manchester. Red Bank Carriage sidings and Newton Heath shed, I'd known them all myself. When we discussed the west coast route via Wigan and Crewe to London and he talked of sweeping into Wigan North Western station braking only twice using vacuum to come to a stand just right for the water column, I knew exactly what he meant, even seeing in my mind the Swan and Royal pub alongside the station. Ken talked of the run to Euston, of Rugby, Willesden, and Camden bank. Again, I had limited knowledge of the run but knew the approach to the capital quite

well, so it all gelled. The era from the 1940's onwards involved local stars like George Formby who lived, at the time, at Beryldene at Singleton (now Kirkstiles) not far from Ken's home in Thornton. There were odd occasions when George escaped briefly the supervision of his overpowering wife Beryl and he would turn up at a pub in Fleetwood only to have her make a dramatic entrance and escort him away. All the thoughts and memories we talked of were never written down, I carried them in my head for over thirty years till I recently talked through them again with Ken and expanded or clarified events for this book. The main stories are told here in the next few pages but throughout the volume we will hear snippets of information and tales as the occasion arises.

Ken was brought up in Burnley on the Colne side of Duke Bar in Randall Street. Leaving school at fourteen, he joined his dad working on the boilers at Mason West and Bathers mill in Harle Syke. Dad was Bert Bradshaw and he'd been in charge of the boiler house there for some 28 years. He'd schooled Ken in looking after 'Lanky' boilers, changing gauge glasses and the like long before he left school, just the way my dad did with me. However, ours were oil fed and Ken's were coal fired and the two boilers there burned twenty three ....*continued on page 10*

....................*continued on page 10*

BLACKPOOL AND FLEETWOOD IN THE 1940'S

FLEETWOOD, 24F		L M S				E.R.O. 23449
	Station	Turn No.				
Engine due to leave Loco. at		m.	Days booked to work			
Trip No.	Dep. Time	From	Arrival Time	Route	Description of Train	Loaded, Empty, L.E. or E.V

Blackpool North Stabling.

	LE	6.10	Shed	Blackpool Nth.
M987	EC	6.50	Blackpool N.	Wyre Dock
	LE		Wyre Dock	Blackpool Nth.
M977	EC	7 55	Blackpool N.	Wyre Dock
	LE		Wyre Dock	Shed.

J E Preston 15/86

continued from page 8..................tons of coal each day. Two years on and Bert was offered a position in charge of the boilers at the new I.C.I. plant, Hillhouse, at Thornton Cleveleys. The family moved to number 12, Hargate Road, Thornton. It was hoped that the move would improve Ken's mum's health. Young Ken took a job on the footplate at Fleetwood Loco, and, yes, this is the way Ken always describes the depot at Wyre Dock. War was looming and eventually came in 1939. The Hillhouse plant became strategic to the war effort, making noxious gases such as phosgene and the like, and Bert could look out from the boiler house window across the railway and a short field to his back door and keep a check that the black-out curtains were drawn at night. Ken, on the other hand was thrown in at the deep end. As a keen reliable fireman he often ended up doing stretches on the London expresses, lodging during the blitz on London. So there you have it, this then is the setting for our coverage of Ken's years on the railway during World War II. It all helps to set the period for the run through to the 1950's where our journeys to the Lancashire coast began. In recent years I made a move to Leeds, though its now no longer the North Eastern region any more and began working via the Calder Valley and Copy Pit to Blackpool North. Hardly a week goes by without making two or three trips and I know that on every one of these journeys, Ken's never been far out of my thoughts, especially as we leave Preston at Maudlands Junction, at Lea Road and again at Poulton. Leaving here, I always look across as we climb to Carleton Crossing, from where you can see the remains of the power plant and I.C.I. works at nearby Thornton. I hear Ken's voice and picture him loading up his pipe from a tobacco pouch. It is all so atmospheric and comforting to have known people like this.

Ken's footplate work included covering the expresses in the war years with Harry Wilkinson, the only Fleetwood man who 'knew' London. He had a bungalow at Broadwater and was lovely quiet man who preached at Sunday School when the chance arose. In wartime there were freight specials to Willesden and sealed orders jobs from Chorley R.O.F. to Crewe in the run up to D-day. Fish traffic also took Ken to London, working the 2/50pm fish out of Wyre Dock to Willesden for Broad Street; it always had 52 vans on. There were three trains in all to Broad Street, the others left at 7pm and 10pm, the latter only if required in later years. The 8.4am passenger to Manchester was the morning businessmans train into town. Local passenger workings were extensive until the advent of the diesel railcars. Some fourteen 'Lanky' tanks were based at Fleetwood for these duties. By the early 1950's, all but a couple were stored as the more modern Ivatt tanks had arrived. There were seasonal boat train specials and again in the early 1950's, the Isle of Man boats were heaving during the summer period between July and September each year, just the way it had been in the 1930's. The fish trade kept busy in those years, creating a lot of rail traffic and shunt turns. On the freight side, coal came from Yorkshire and the Wigan area for the boats, as well as the power stations, soda works and Hillhouse plant at Burn Naze and Thornton. The trains Ken worked from the ammonia soda works left at about midnight, journeying via the west coast route to Wembley for Sudbury. Other night jobs included coal empties to Rose Grove, Brindle Heath, Wigan and Aintree.

The war years made a big impression on Ken. He was in his late teens as the war started and was firing to London as the Germans nightly bombed the East End. He worked with various drivers at this time, Harry Wilkinson as mentioned, Jack Fleetwood was another. Jack one night refused to leave the lodge house to go to the shelters during the bombing managing somehow to sleep through it all. During those dark days the expresses had original boilered Royal Scots on them and 'Lizzies' as well as the coal miners friend, the 5X's (Jubilees) and Patriot class engines. Ken would often sign on at night and go light engine with sealed orders which were only opened and read once they'd gotten well away from the shed. They would go to Chorley and take bombs on to Crewe or the docks. Having worked a shift firing, he would at times arrive on shed in the evening and be told to take up fire watch duties for the next twelve hours. They used little old coaches by the shed for this and on numerous occasions he would clamber on the roof to look out across the water watching the Germans bomb Barrow in Furness. 'Gerry' would have flown over Fleetwood on their way to Barrow, having first been to Liverpool. Ken and Harry Wilkinson were chased by the Germans late one night as they headed home to Fleetwood light engine. Harry heard them above and told Ken to keep the fire hole shut. They kept going all the way from Singleton to Wyre Dock before the aircraft veered away out to sea. Even so, Harry wouldn't allow Ken to deal with the fire until they were sure the plane wasn't coming back. At least two bombs fell on the nearby salt marshes as the 'Gerry's' were being chased by the allies. The area where the bombs fell is now full of caravans as part of the Carla Gran campsite. Another of Ken's jobs over the years was transporting thousands of tons of cotton waste for dumping into the marshes near Wyre Dock to reclaim the land.

It was Ned Whiteside who taught Ken to drive. An old 'Lanky' man, one of the old school, but one who looked after his young mates. Ken was with Ned when he slid into the buffers at Blackpool North. You dropped into the platforms at the North station and then the line levelled as you ran towards the buffers. On this occasion, Ned began to slide as he braked ready to come to a stand. He wound the engine quickly into back gear....too late though and they came to rest mounted on the Ticket Inspectors hut, part of which was now demolished. Apparently they had been unloading fish, and fish gravy and slime was covering the rail top. Once when Ken had a 'stinker' of a cold, Ned made him go to the Isle of Man boat that had just berthed and ask the crew who knew Ned to give Ken two pair of best Manx kippers. Back on the engine, Ned got Ken to scrape the butter off his bread and place it in the bowl of the firing shovel and then cook the kippers in the firehole. He made Ken eat a full pair of kippers to himself. They certainly shifted the cold.

(Above) Just as Ken remembers them. This is one of the Blackpool 'Lanky' Radial tanks standing in platform No. 5 at the North station. To a great extent it is just like those shedded at Fleetwood that Ken would work to and fro on the push pull trains. Engine No. **10721** however, isn't motor fitted, there are no Westinghouse fittings visible here and Fleetwood motor trains tended to have the engine leading into Blackpool. Nevertheless, the old girl looks the part and seen here under the North station roof, it is a picture that is bound to stir memories. The date is probably the late 1940's, as by 1950 most of the Blackpool 'Lanky' tanks were in store on the North shed with little in the way of a future. *Authors collection*

GOOD MATES ..... AND BAD ONES

If Ned Whiteside was the former, then Jack Swarbrick was the latter. Full of his own importance he would always try to put his young mates down in front of those in charge, but they invariably could see through him. He was headstrong and totally set in his manner. Some lads obliged him and drew his oil and warmed it on the throat plate just to keep the peace but Ken wouldn't play that game. When Ken refused to do it, Swarbrick asked for a fresh fireman. The running shift foreman said, *'That best tek 'im with thee, wi'th getten nobody else. Thyl hav to warm thee own oil today* !..........

On another outing with Jack Swarbrick, Ken was on the local push-pull trips, and

between trips whilst stood at Fleetwood station, Ken decided to get the coal down and break some up for later. He had forgotten Swarbrick always placed his tea bottle through the spy glass hole and rested it on the coal pile in the bunker, Crash…! Ken had stuck the coal pick through Jack's bottle. Swarbrick was away telling the tale, so Ken nipped smartly up to the 'refresh' on the concourse and asked the lasses there if they could fix him up with a pop bottle like Jack's and fill it with cold tea, minus milk of course. Ken dashed back and placed the bottle back on the coal and awaited events. Sure enough, out came the bottle and Jack placed it behind the injector pipe

to warm up as Ken watched him anxiously. Once warmed through, Swarbrick grabbed the bottle, took the top off and had a drink, then sticking out his chest said, *'Do you know Ken, my wife makes the best tea in Fleetwood* !..........

WARTIME AT THE WINTER GARDENS

(Above) The Empress ballroom at Blackpool's Winter Gardens was the resorts largest dance floor. As well as a stage for the band it boasted a mighty Wurlitzer organ like the one played at the Tower ballroom by Reginald Dixon. Horace Finch was the organist at the Empress ballroom for many years. Over at the Palace ballroom back in the 1940's, the area around the edge of the dance floor was covered in large coloured glass squares which were illuminated from beneath, all very modern. **(below)** When he wasn't entertaining our lads abroad on the war fronts, George Formby was making box office smashes for the cinema. In the film seen here (Spare a Copper), George is chatting up his co-star Dorothy Hyson. Apparently he asked her one day to come back to his dressing room for a bit of fun. When she replied that she didn't do that sort of thing, he simply said *'Ha well lets go and have a cup of tea instead'*…………

Blackpool during the Second World War

Blackpool during the war years was somewhat over-run with allied personnel, mainly the R.A.F. and American airmen based at the surrounding airfields and camps and billeted in the many guest houses and hotels. Some three quarters of a million men received their basic training at the Winter Gardens. Despite the war, life went on the dance halls and pubs still opened. Young and old alike still wanted to make the best of it in those dark days. Ken Bradshaw mated around with another fireman the mighty Arthur 'tiny' Calvert. At slightly above 6ft 3ins tall, 'Tiny' towered above the 5ft 6in of Ken. They usually toured around town calling at the popular haunts of the time like the Manchester Hotel on the Central promenade. Always heaving with servicemen ready for action, there was much taunting of Ken and his mates by the 'Brylcreem' boys deriding the valuable footplate work they did in reserved occupations. Ken at times went outside and fisticuffs ensued and if need be the large frame of 'Tiny' Calvert was put to good use, seeing things didn't get too much out of hand. Ken always liked to visit the Palace varieties and as we see to the right below it was still a good show into the early 1950's. Top singing star of the day Ronnie Hilton has been secured for the odd Sunday night concert which no doubt would be a 'sell-out' given his popularity at the time. Above (left) we see the platform at St. Annes. A mixture of American and R.A.F airmen are seen dancing at the Winter Gardens in the view below (left). Finally, Dave Morris (shown topping the bill at the Palace), was a popular longstanding personality, particularly remembered hosting his 'Club Night' on Central pier in the immediate post-war years.

DRIVER LAURIE EARL
of CAMDEN

"SERVICE"
TIMEKEEPER WATCHES

Whilst on loan in the war years, and probably just after, Ken Bradshaw worked, as required, under emergency workings. However, once things settled down and after the war, Blackpool men had a turn number 60 which worked the 5.5pm Blackpool Central to Euston arriving at 11/04pm. They backed the stock out and went to Camden shed with the loco, for 12.7am, then lodged, taking an engine off the shed at 11.40am and, depending on the years, either worked to Crewe or went 'as-pass' before having a break and heading home working the 4/40pm to Blackpool (W243), getting relieved upon arrival. It was whilst on these jobs that Ken came into contact with the infamous Driver Earl of Camden depot. He was a legend in terms of time keeping, so much so that he endorsed the range of 'Service' brand timekeeper watches. He had started on the railway back in LNWR days and knew the main line with his eyes shut, but to keep time in the manner which he did and in view of the many restrictions on trackwork and structures following the war years, Earl would thrash engines unmercifully to prove a point and in doing so hammered his mates as well. If you happened to be piloted by Driver Earl, then as train engine you could expect a rough ride to say the least. On the day that Ken had with him, Driver Earl, having backed up on Ken's engine in the platform at Euston, jumped down and strode down the platform with his usual swagger and proceeded to lay the law down to Ken's driver, the ever quiet and genial Harry Wilkinson. Harry stopped his banter and quietly said, *'Mr Earl, when we get to the troughs en route, you take the front half and we'll have the rear, is that clear?'*. Off strode Earl in bullish fashion. Earl got 'at em' from the start, hammer and tongs, fireworks galore, and when the first water troughs were dipped, Earl took the lot. Harry Wilkinson turned to Ken and said, *'Put some coal on, fill thee boiler and shut the damper, he can pull us to Crewe'*, and he did. Upon arrival at Crewe, Driver Earl wasted no time in jumping off and fairly came bouncing back towards Ken and Harry all red and flustered, but backed off when Harry said, *'Look, you took the water we needed, what did you expect?'*. Soon after in 1947 Driver Earl retired to write his memoirs.

Time for a change. Around the 1957/58 period, Ken was increasingly unhappy with the job, the diesels were coming. It seemed as if there was a serious possibility that many trains would become single manned in time. The railcars were just the start of something far greater. Ken could not really see life on the expresses or even the locals without steamers on the front. A lot of the older drivers he had known had now retired and there was a feeling of isolation setting in. The local Union 'Rep' Harry Porter found out the way Ken felt and suggested Ken have a ride to Preston on the new railcar they were using for training. The idea was to show Ken what was involved. Ken drove back but wasn't impressed one bit. In fact the trip made his mind up quicker if anything and the offer of

a house in Nelson clinched it. Despite being asked to consider a move to Rose Grove, Ken declined and left the railway in 1958. It was things like maintenance, or rather the lack of it, which worried Ken, pushing washout limits and the like. It was all a risky game. One day working to Crewe with a boat train special, a gauge glass blew on the footplate (they go with a hell of a bang). The Driver George Arthur Smith took his jacket off and quickly threw it over it to kill the steam and water spray. No sooner had he done that than the other one went bang, what a day. **(top left)** We can see the entrance to Euston station from platforms one and two. Top right is Driver Billy Barlow who gave Ken quite a surprise one night at Preston. Ken's house in Burnley backed onto Billy's,

and as kids they were best mates, Ken though always knew him as 'Willy'. The friendship ended when Ken moved to Thornton. One night the Perth man ran into the back of the London-Blackpool as it stood waiting a platform at Ribble Sidings at Preston. The driver was shaken up and asked for relief. Ken was sent out to drive for him and climbing up on to the engine in the dark he was gobsmacked to see by the glow of the fire Willy Barlow sitting in the firemans seat. He had no idea that for years they'd both been on the footplate based at depots just miles apart from each other. Lastly, Ken is seen in the cab of **43025** backing onto Crewe North shed, possibly having been asked to take the engine light from London rather than going passenger to Crewe.

At the end of World War II when Ken Bradshaw was still working the odd London turn and covering the Broad Street fish trains through to Willesden, a young Archie Buchanan was a junior in the laboratory at the Ammonia Soda works at Burn Naze. Always mad keen on the railways, well he would be, his dad had been a station master locally for some years. At the age of seventeen, Archie joined the LMS at Fleetwood MPD as an engine cleaner. Old enough to do shifts,

he was, within six weeks, passed out as a passed cleaner which included disposing of engines on the shed, and firing turns locally. The railway in those post war years was desperately short of men in many departments. By 1948 he was firing to Crewe, amongst other places, gaining a week alongside Driver Billy Greenwood working the 2/50pm Broad Street fish train to Crewe; twice that week they had Royal Scot engines with their original boilers. One of these was **6113**

Cameronian (see below). National service then intervened and it was the summer of 1950 when Archie got back to Fleetwood. Straight back into firing he spent the rest of the summer on the locals firing for Bill 'Pompey' Collinson. They are seen above on the platform at Fleetwood together with the station foreman, a shunter and the trolley girls from the 'refresh' (Archie's the one on the left side). Fireman at the shed Ken 'Busker' Watson took the picture. Archie was lucky really working on

ARCHIE BUCHANAN
FIREMAN AT FLEETWOOD AND WILLESDEN

the old 'Lanky' tanks as it was about the last year they were used in any numbers on these local services. Getting itchy feet, Archie went on loan to Saltley then quickly to a more permanent position at Willesden. Working up to Crewe on lodge jobs, he would relieve his old mates on the 2/50 fish, taking it through to Broad Street on another Willesden trip turn.

The life at Willesden was good, the work varied and intensive. He even worked the ammonia soda trains from Burn Naze, from the works where he'd started off as a junior in the offices. He had worked them through to Canning Town in the East End of London with drivers from Willesden shed. Regretably, events which took place on the 23rd July 1952 robbed Archie of the career he was carving out. Entering Leighton Buzzard station one day with a Stanier class eight loco, hauling a lengthy empty wagon train from Brent, he was catapulted over the back of the tender after being caught by a wire stretching across the platforms that was positioned little higher than train height. Despite falling down between the tender and the first wagon, he came to rest sitting upright and facing forward. His driver had stopped in good time but Archie's legs were shattered in the fall and had he not been taken to the Royal Buckinghamshire Hospital in Aylesbury where they had the latest methods of treatment, he feels sure one of the legs

would have been lost. It was a long road back to recovery. Plastic surgery was needed and time was spent in Stoke Mandeville hospital. Eighteen months on he was back in Thornton and back at work but only in the lodge house on Central Drive at Blackpool, cooking and preparing breakfasts for up to 40 men a day. The railway doctor wouldn't pass him fit for the footplate despite the shortage of men; surely he could have handled the shunt turns. He talked it over with his dad who suggested young Archie should consider a move in to the traffic department and become a signalman. This sounded okay. Soon, Archie was training at Layton signalbox. In 1955, he was working temporary at the new Wyre Power station cabin and did spells at Morecambe's Torresholme No. 1 and at Heysham Harbour. Then to Treales near Kirkham to work with Alf Jolly. He would 'push-bike' from home in Thornton all the way to Treales, so why he wasn't allowed on the footplate is a mystery. Ken Bradshaw recalls Archie being in Burn Naze North signal box in the later 1950's and he did a summer in Poulton's No.1 box before moving to Blackpool to Blackpool South No. 3; He worked for a while at Spen Dyke by the engine sheds before moving back to Blackpool South where his career ended on the railway about the time steam finished. The railway on the Fylde had contracted out of all proportion by then.

(Above) As part of a running-in turn from Crewe, immaculate Rebuilt 'Scot' **46103** *Royal Scots Fusilier*, works the 2/50 fish past Stanley Hill on 4th April 1960. *Peter Fitton*

Pictures on these pages by *Archie Buchanan, Peter Fitton and Stuart Taylor*

Our starting point. Our glimpse of the lives of railwaymen Ken Bradshaw and Archie Buchanan have helped to move our story along from the war years to the 1950's where my family outings began. The 1950's were still all about making do and mend, fancy goods and luxuries like we have today were unknown. Good enter-

SUMMER 1956

tainment and enjoyable holidays could be had quite cheaply if you did your sums right. Whilst a feeling of austerity seemed ever apparent there also was an over-whelming feeling of relief. Having lived with so much uncertainty in life during the war years people of all ages seemed, as the '50's progressed, to be making more of life and by the end of the decade, young as we may have been, I truly sensed changes taking place with each holiday year. Those changes seem to speed up as we entered the 1960's. Why I logged those changes in my mind, what they actually meant and why I can still recount the senses and feel of those years over forty years later is something I cannot explain but it certainly helps when putting these books togeth-er. The war atmosphere didn't end in 1945 or 1950, as dad was called up for Z training at Weymouth when the Korean conflict took place in 1953. Thankfully he didn't have to go. In 1956 the silly politicions took us again to the brink of full scale war over the Suez Canal affair. That all began to gather pace in late July and the autumn of 1956. Our annual holidays, July 8th to the 20th that

year went off okay. Those were still the years of red and cream coaches and the older era of engines like the 'Lanky' tall funnelled tanks and 'A' class tender engines shuffling about the local railways. We'd see the 'Super D' 0-8-0's on our out-ing to Lakeside lined up on Carnforth shed not knowing quite what class they were, but they sure looked Victorian. I remember trying to grasp just what was all the fuss about singer Johnny Ray. He was touring Britain at summer. Why did the girls go all funny whenever his music was playing and wherever we seemed to be his wailing voice wasn't far away from us at the Lancashire resorts that 1956 season. **(above)** Two months after our outings to Blackpool, the annual Evereds social club specials from Birmingham wended their way along from Preston. The first, train 'A' is seen passing Kirkham and Wesham on Saturday the 8th September 1956. Two or three trains were needed in all and they continued running into the 1960's.

KIRKHAM AND WESHAM

Gateway to the Fylde Coast

On the platform, 29th September 1956. There should have been four platforms at Kirkham and Wesham. The fast lines were remodelled prior to the war in readiness for the upgrading of services and new lengthy platforms capable of taking the longest trains were planned. Blackpool North's new concrete excursion platforms buildings were another of the 1930's upgrades but the platforms at Kirkham never happened, the war intervened and the project was never revived post-war. **(above)** B1 No. **61256** heads for Blackpool with special 774 from Boston as local engine **45212** sets off for Colne with the first of its two trips to East Lancashire that day. Kirkham's South Junction signal box is visible in the middle of the picture.

(left) The fireman of B1 No. **61080** must clearly think he needs a big fire on to get across the Marton, either that or he has a hell of a train on. Excursion 762 was from Hull as was the engine.

KIRKHAM
AND WESHAM

Kirkham and Wesham, the changing scene. Two views here show just how much of a change Kirkham's island platform would see in little over a decade. **(above) 73026** came new to Blackpool Central, stayed a short while then travelled around the country, being based at Tyseley for a while, by which time the livery had gone from black to lined green. As we will see in the reprise book (*SFTP 26/6*), the engine came to Blackpool North with a Tyseley crew and in time came to Bolton with another green Standard Five 73014. Both these engines appear in the reprise on excursions to the North station. In this 1950's scene, it is Rigby Road man Ernie McClusky looking out of the fireman's side. By contrast we have a picture taken in 1965 (August), of **44930** on a Liverpool working. The platform awning has gone and there's an air of rationalisation about the place. Pictures *Stuart Taylor* and *Paul Claxton*.

Passing through. In the hectic excursion years of the 1950's and up to about 1962, Kirkham was the ideal spotting place. Everything heading to the coast, whichever route it was taking, had to pass by you. The cobbled road leading to the goods yard was right by the line side. It was brilliant for picture taking as we can see in these two scenes. **(above)** By the 1960's, catching any of the poppet valve 'Crabs' working was a real treat. Easter Monday 1960 saw two of them reach Blackpool North (18/4/60). Special No. 972 clatters by the goods yard with **42824** on the front end. Eight coaches was an average load for a 'Crab'. The ten coaches behind 42824 would therefore need that extra effort and no doubt cause the engine to get a 'waddle' on at times. **(below)** Coming out of Blackpool is the Sheffield (1E47) in the days before the diesels quickly took charge of this service. Brian Hyland, together with brother Peter and the other lads from Low Moor, were booked to work this back to Mirfield in steam days off a Friday night lodge job to Fleetwood when the Isle of Man TT races were on. Pictures by *Peter Fitton* and *Arnold Battson.*

SEASIDE, EVENING AND OTHER EXCURSIONS To BLACKPOOL

Blackpool bound. (left-upper) A very tidy looking **45674** *Duncan* rolls cautiously towards the North Junction at Kirkham awaiting a run to Blackpool. With thirteen coaches in tow, the fireman will certainly be ready for a break having travelled all the way from Arley with 1T09. The breeze out on the Marton will no doubt perk him up no end. On the left is Parkinson's biscuit works, now Fox's. (above) Working the 'locals' to Liverpool is **75049**. These 'Standard Fours' were very familiar running into and out of Blackpool. They rarely had time to go sit on the shed at Rigby Road. A quick turn on the table, clean the fire, get water and have quick brew and a sandwich and it was off again for another trip. **(page23-below)** Looking back towards Kirkham and Wesham from the overbridge by the goods yard, we see the celebrated '2/50 fish' from Wyre Dock to Broad Street (London). **45369** is the engine today to Crewe and in need of a washout by the looks of it. Passing him on the Down Fast line is a north line trip freight with 48295 which appears almost ex works. Pictures by *Chris Spring*, *Peter Fitton* and *Paul Claxton*.

(Above/top - Page 24) Kirkham North Junction, 20th July 1963. We are now looking the other way towards the coast and Blackpool from the goods yard bridge. It is exactly six and three quarter miles looking straight ahead to Blackpool Tower. Things here seem quiet as they were at times, but on other occasions these rails would be occupied every few minutes with trains queuing to take one of the three routes into Blackpool. Excursion trains would often back up to Lea Road at busy times. All would be champing at the bit eager to get there and most crews in the summer would be looking forward to a pint or two for it was one of the few pleasures that awaited them at the seaside. The yard on the left held some 423 wagons, the goods yard nearer the station holding another 116 wagon lengths. The marshalling yard sidings, being very long, proved ideal for the storage of carriages from incoming excursions. These were tripped out and back at various times of the day and night as required. The lines curving away to the left go round the coast line. Straight on takes you onto the Marton line and those to the right go to Poulton for Fleetwood and Blackpool North. BR Standard Class 6MT No 72006 Clan McKenzie has just reached the 40mph board on the Up Fast entering Kirkham and 1S28 is the Blackpool North - Glasgow service. (Above/right lower - Page 24) In 1957 a presentation was held at the Railway Hotel upon the retirement of one of the Kirkham signalmen. Seen amongst the gentlemen are :- at the front, Harry Southern-Preston Control (glasses) then the chap retiring whose name we don't have, then on the right is Ernie Seed, J.P. from Poulton No.3 nicknamed 'old pal'. In the middle are Tommy Poynton (Kirkham North Jnc) and Ken Cartmell from Salwick. At the back-in the middle-is Ted Dickinson, relief man, and young Archie Buchanan, who was by then at Burn Naze North signal box, is on the right.

Pictures by *Paul Claxton* and *Archie Buchanan*.

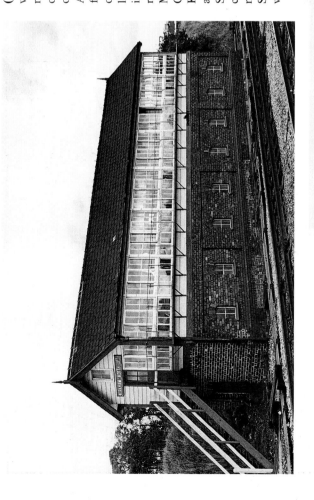

KIRKHAM NORTH JUNCTION

(Above-left) Kirkham North Junction cabin. Nowadays one of the few remaining structures still surviving on the route to Blackpool, the North Junction Signal box was always manned by good keen signalmen who knew just how to regulate trains and keep the job moving. They tended to know which drivers they could trust if they gave them 'a run', they would lean out of the box window and wag their finger at the driver, this advised him to make 'a point'. The driver would respond whistling and waving acknowledgement and then they were off. If you worked in the next day and you had shown willing then the signalman got you away in good time and that is the way it worked. Good railway work by all concerned. (right) 42832 was a memorable refugee from Scotland. It had the large cab side numbers and is seen here on the 1/25pm Burn Naze - Corkickle Soda Ash train on the 12th September 1964. It was written off at Blackburn Taylor street after a collision involving the Heysham – Hollins oil train in 1965. Picture by *Peter Fitton*.

KIRKHAM NORTH JUNCTION

BRADKIRK

Kirkham to Bradkirk.

(Page 26-above) 1M51 takes the Marton line on the 20th July 1963. Farnley's ex-works 5X No. **45695** *Minotaur* is working the 8.17am excursion from Morley Low to Blackpool Central and passing Kirkham at 10.50am. The coast line is seen curving away to the right and there are the marshalling yard sidings which at one time acted as overspill carriage sidings. **(Above-this page)** Rose Grove's **42898,** in fine form, speeds under the flyover at Bradkirk with 1T83, a special from Accrington to Fleetwood on 17th May 1964. Over on the right **(this page)**, light engine **42863** approaches Bradkirk signal box and is taking the line over the flyover onto the Up Fast as it heads towards Kirkham on 27th July 1963. It had worked in from Shipley. Pictures by *Paul Claxton* and *Peter Fitton.*

TAKING THE NORTH LINE

Now we are on our way, taking the north line to Poulton for Blackpool North and Fleetwood. (above) On the 3rd of April 1962, Fleetwood engine **42842** makes steady progress at Bradkirk with the 11.15am Brindle Heath to Wyre Dock freight which includes a number of empty fish vans. The modern Insulfish vans, with their wide wheelbase and roller bearings were well liked by operating staff and the bodies were lined inside with stainless steel. Some were made as late as 1962; Beeching axed the fish traffic less than three years later. (right) Bridge 29 was the footbridge at Bradkirk and from here you also had a great view of the two routes to Blackpool. The Marton line is on the left and the north line to the right. Excursion trains could be seen chasing each other neck and neck along here for about a mile before the routes widened and disappeared through different bridge holes near Weeton and Plumpton. 42842 picture by *Chris Spring*.

1X42 to Blackpool North. It is Whit Sunday, 10th of June 1962 and it turned out to be the last big day ever of excursion trains into Blackpool. Some 50 specials arrived that morning. This one brought the ultra rare **45607** *Fiji* from Sheffield Millhouses shed with an outing from Heckmondwike. Go put the kettle on as this lot takes some reading!....The first to pass was 42709 at 10.25am with 1T59 from Manchester. At 10.30am, 44889 brought 1T58 from Church and Oswaldtwistle. Six minutes behind them was 42716 from Colne (1T57), all three taking the Marton route. At 10.38am, 75046 working the Liverpool Exchange to Blackpool North service train came by on the North line. Next to pass was 1Z46 Birches head gardners special from Hanley on the Marton line at 10.41am. 42838 followed him on the Marton with 1T70 from Darwen. Nearly ten minutes then passed until 46109 *Royal Engineer* also took the Marton line with 1X09 from Bradford. 42714 on 1T80 from Pendleton was only four minutes behind the 'Scot' on the Marton and just three minutes behind him was 44713 with 1Z31 from Blythe Bridge. Another ten minutes went by before 42820 on a Rochdale – Blackpool special came by (1T82). Two Black Fives were next; 45060 on 1Z33 over the Marton which was a Burslem Co-op special, No. 2 from Newchapel and Golden Hill. 45002 then took 1Z17 from Stoke to Blackpool North, passing at 11.17am. Taking the Marton line at the same time rattling along light engine was 75048. At 11.23am, a B1 No. 61295 took the North line with 1X10 from Wakefield. Six minutes on and Lower Darwen driver Albert Fletcher came dashing under the footbridge at Bradkirk going over the Marton line with 1T65 from Blackburn (see the front inlay of part three in the series); the engine was 76083. On the Up and crossing the flyover at 11.35am was 44895. At 11.44am the whistling of a E.E. type 4 brought D210 on the north line

with a passenger service from Manchester. Right behind him but going over the Marton was 1T85 from Skipton using 45154 *Lanarkshire Yeomanry*. 1T21 took the north route at 11.53am with 61011 on a special from Hadfield. Also going Blackpool North was 44873 from Walsall (1Z60) at 11.56am. Only 4 minutes behind him to Poulton was 44937 with 1Z35 from Silverdale. Next for the Marton was 1T83 from Settle with 45435. Then, an old favourite came by, 45581 *Bihar and Orissa* from Leeds City South (1X88) went forward via the Marton line, closely followed by 44694 with 1T86, an excursion from Todmorden. 45203, as you would expect, came past with 1T78 from Manchester, also on the Marton route. The second Farnley 5X was 45646 *Napier* going to the North with the A.E.U. special from Leeds City North. Three minutes behind him on the North line was another 5X 45722 *Defence* (2A) on 1Z61 from Darleston.Two Brush type 2's rawting away brought the special 1X21 by from Rotherham Masboro'. Along the Down Marton line at 12/23pm, D5826 and D5821 were the locos. Right up behind them was 45233 from Diggle (1Z32) and 1Z37 from Uttoxeter came by 42769 going on the North line with 45048 at 12/30pm. There was still an hour and a quarter to go. Another Sheffield area special was D5814 from Ecclesfield 1X13 (Marton line). Chasing him was an old 'Crab' 42768 from Kearsley (1T72). Wakefield's 61161 followed them four minutes later with 1X36 from Ossett. On the Up from Blackpool North was 75046 going back to Liverpool at 12/39pm. Passing it at Kirkham North Junction was 42706, once the pride of Rose Grove, working 1T63 to the North from Accrington. Shed mate 42717 was next on the Marton (1T67) from Burnley at 12/45pm. Two minutes after on the North route was the cop of the day 45607 *Fiji* and 1X42. 44990 was right behind him with

1X41 from Bradford, and chasing him was 61385 with 1X15 from Castleford. 46129 *The Scottish Horse* took the flyover on the Up line at 12/57pm LE; 1Z42 was 3x2 Car railcars from Carlisle via the Marton, then there was a gap of eleven minutes before 45536 followed them with 1T79 from Oldham. 45088, a Saltley engine, brought 1T20 (Northfield) along the Down North line at 1/10pm. Right up behind him, getting checked at Weeton, was 45093 from Warrington (1Z43). An empty stock 3T81 took the flyover on the Up from the Marton with 42436. Passing him and skirting the flyover was 45689 *Ajax* from Trent (1T09). Chased by 45211 on the Leeds City south excursion, 45001 brought the Etruria special 1Z76 along the North line and trying hard to catch him up was 42896 on 1T06 from Nottingham. Two separate Brush type 2's then came on the Marton, D5689 with 1X22 from Sheffield and D5837 (1X34) ex Chesterfield. The last 5X to come was 45567 *South Australia* at 1/33pm with 1Z66 from Birmingham. As he dashed along the north line, 45391 tried to keep up with him on the Down Marton line with 1Z36 from Macclesfield. 73161 on 1X90 (Woodlesford) near Stourton also went to the North at 1/36pm followed closely by 42898 with 1T69 from Colne. The last steamers were a treat, Doncaster B1's 61365 and 61360 double headed the 1X12 special in from 'Donny' that day. Apparently, the previous year (21st May 1961) Doncaster had turned out K3 61899 to Blackpool with 12 coaches on !.....and it struggled and arrived late. No wonder, the crew should have had gallant service medals for that one. As the B1's trotted on the North line and all fell quiet, D210 whistled its way back along the Up North line back to Manchester. The picture of 45607 is by *Paul Claxton*.

Weeton Lane bridge. As the North line ran parallel with the Marton route from Bradkirk they gradually moved further apart until Weeton was reached about a mile from Bradkirk. It was here that the North line dipped slightly into Weeton cutting. Weeton Lane overbridge spanned that cutting and the line curved steadily to the right on the run round to Singleton Bank. Weeton signal cabin, a famous little structure, was perched high above the cutting by the lane side. **(above) 44803** is en route to Manchester on a gloriously sunny Saturday morning (2nd July 1966). *Paul Claxton.*

(left) Weeton signal box. As we will read shortly, the little cabin here was to play a part in the unfortunate collision in July 1961 involving an Isle of Man boat train and a heavy ballast train that had been working overnight. The incident was very much a one-off, and considering the thousands of train movements over these routes during the season, all done safely, it understandably upset the highly conscious signalmen who covered the work in these local signal boxes. It is never just one factor which causes an accident such as this, usually it's a number of events coming together which set the course for disaster. **Over on page 31** we see **90722** coming along Weeton cutting from the direction of Singleton Bank. The lengthy train of empties for the Yorkshire coal fields will need lifting a bit here up the slight grade towards Bradkirk hence the fireman's freshly charged fire.

Engineer's possession

Ballast workings, cleaning and replacing ballast, changing rails, as well as turning them, together with tamping and lining were all done under an engineer's possession of the lines as time permitted, over the weekend or odd nights during the week. The working was usually safe but the tendency to over-run the allotted time did cause stress and panic at times. Ballast cleaning, using a proper machine, large spoil trains and tamping machines was scheduled on the Up line between Singleton and Weeton over the Saturday night/Sunday morning period during July of 1961. Over the weekend of the 8th and 9th of July, work had been done satisfactorily. The same type of work was planned for the 15th and 16th of July but unfortunately on this occasion all did not go well. Work began on the Saturday night and progressed into Sunday morning of the 16th July. At 8.50am, the Permanent Way Inspector in charge, having worked the Down line towards Poulton as a single line over which trains could move in both directions under pilot man's supervision, decided to withdraw the single line order and begin moving the ballast trains off the work site in readiness for the coming days special excursions and service trains that would be needing to use the route into Blackpool. As he withdrew the order, he advised the Weeton signalman that he would take the loaded waste ballast train, now standing on the Down line at Singleton Bank, forward to Poulton once the workmen had finished loading and shutting the wagon doors. Passed fireman J. Dean was in charge of a Class 8 loco, hauling the thirty-nine wagons of spent ballast and a brake van that day in 1961. Still at work on the 'dead' Up road were a spoil train, a large ballast cleaner, and a tamping machine. These would all have to proceed in convoy towards Singleton signal box and wait to cross over onto the Down line to run to Poulton to be stabled one at a time. The point where the work was being carried out was near to Singleton Bank signal box, which was effectively switched out of use at that time. The inspector should really only have stopped briefly to sort the wagons out and then set off for Singleton. Instead, he allowed the work gang to continue to load spoil, thus making the job over-run. It was now well after 10am and excursion trains and the like were heading for Blackpool and Fleetwood. Seasonal boat special 1P29 had left Colne for Fleetwood at 8.50am with an heavy schedule of stops to Preston, all stations via Accrington. It was formed of 3x2 cars of the new Cravens DMU sets based at Accrington, but now often out stabled at Colne carriage sidings. M50808 and M50783 were leading, with M51780 and M51755 in the middle and M51771 together with M51746 bringing up the rear. The new units had only recently taken over the running of the passenger services to and from Blackpool from the steamers and coaching stock. Another point to dwell on is that these boat trains would cease to run in September when the landing stage at Fleetwood was condemned. By the time the boat train from

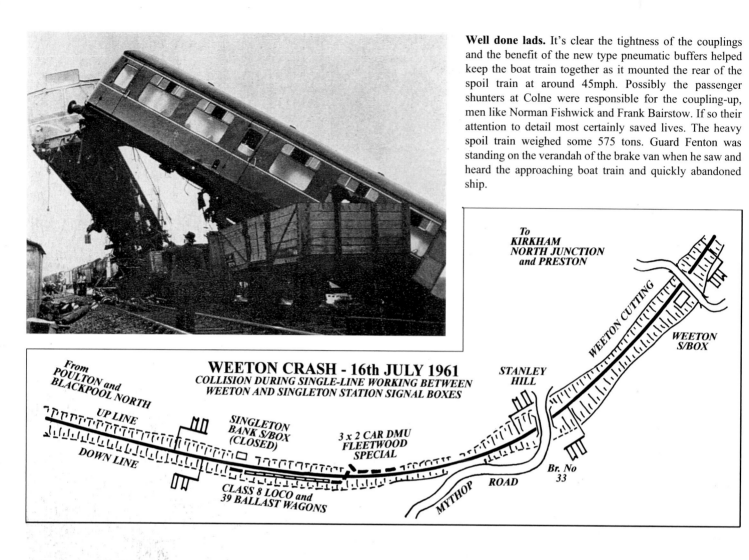

Well done lads. It's clear the tightness of the couplings and the benefit of the new type pneumatic buffers helped keep the boat train together as it mounted the rear of the spoil train at around 45mph. Possibly the passenger shunters at Colne were responsible for the coupling-up, men like Norman Fishwick and Frank Bairstow. If so their attention to detail most certainly saved lives. The heavy spoil train weighed some 575 tons. Guard Fenton was standing on the verandah of the brake van when he saw and heard the approaching boat train and quickly abandoned ship.

To
**KIRKHAM
NORTH JUNCTION
and PRESTON**

WEETON CUTTING

**WEETON
S/BOX**

WEETON CRASH - 16th JULY 1961
*COLLISION DURING SINGLE-LINE WORKING BETWEEN
WEETON AND SINGLETON STATION SIGNAL BOXES*

**STANLEY
HILL**

**From
POULTON and
BLACKPOOL NORTH**

UP LINE

**SINGLETON
BANK S/BOX
(CLOSED)**

**3 x 2 CAR DMU
FLEETWOOD
SPECIAL**

DOWN LINE

*Br. No
33*

**CLASS 8 LOCO and
39 BALLAST WAGONS**

MYTHOP ROAD

Colne had reached Preston it was running late and carrying some 346 passengers. Roughly about the same time as the boat train headed out along by Maudland Viaduct leaving Preston, the PW Inspector was holding a telephone conversation with the young signalman at Singleton discussing the removal of the remaining ballast trains still blocking the lines. The young lad working Singleton signal box had only come on duty at 5.30am and had physically not seen any of the trains that were the topic of conversation. It seems that he became confused, believing that a least one spoil train of loaded ballast wagons was leaving the work site by going towards Kirkham. It is possible he came to think that the only ballast trains still in situ were all on the 'closed' Up line. As the pressure and pace of events gathered momentum, the signalman at Weeton entered the proceedings. He was being pressed by Bradkirk to find out what was happening, as the boat train from Colne was due within minutes and already running late. The Weeton

signalman asked the lad at Singleton for a 'line-clear' in order that the he could offer on the 1P29 boat train. Initially the lad at Singleton refused to give a line clear signal on the instruments. Then, as the Weeton signalman tried again and also talked on the phone to Singleton box, the young lad suddenly decided to give a line-clear to Weeton signalbox, even though 39 wagons of spoil were standing halfway between him and Weeton cabin on the Down line into Poulton. The Weeton signalman, upon receiving the 'line-clear', told the flagman to go down and remove the detonator protection on the Down line that was placed along Weeton cutting in advance of Weeton signalbox, in readiness for the boat train to pass. The last safety item capable of halting the boat train in time had been removed. Weeton raised his signals and Driver Shaw in charge of the boat train special apparently accelerated upon seeing the signals raised and sped down Weeton cutting towards Mythop Road bridge at Stanley Hill completely unaware of what lay round the

curve. The loaded spoil train had been slowly moving off towards Singleton but a wagon door had been spotted partly open and the train was halted for the door to be secured. This was happening just as the boat train came round the bend at 10.25am that fateful Sunday morning. Driver Shaw was doing 55-60mph as he took the wide sweeping right hand curve towards Singleton Bank. He would know from his traffic notices about the ballast work and would briefly think, upon seeing the lengthy ballast train ahead, that it was standing the wrong way round over on the opposite line (the Up line). Some 400 yards away, he tragically realised it was in front of him. I sense a little of what he must have felt knowing and working the route myself and having been more than once placed in a position where you knew you couldn't possibly avoid hitting something on the line in front of you. He applied the brake to emergency stayed at his post and blasted on the horn, a brave man indeed and one who lost his life in the process. Six of the 346 passengers lost their lives also and many more were injured as the railcars mounted the brake van and wagons and rode over the top before crashing down into the field below. The second and third coaches were left high in the air but none of the couplings gave way and therefore there was no telescoping of the carriages, which usually causes heavy loss of life. Of the six passengers killed one woman who'd been sitting behind driver Shaw remained unidentified. It turned out the woman was from Colne. She had been going to the Isle of Man for a week's holiday, it was only when she failed to return the following week that neighbours became worried the mystery woman killed at Weeton may well be her. Recovery operations were carried out using steam cranes from Lostock Hall and Newton Heath depots and engines in use were 90541, 45241 and 45002 on the Sunday afternoon. 46449 was at work on the 19th dropping fresh ballast as services were restored and normality returned.

(Right) Singleton signal box. The little cabin seen here was at the Poulton end of the single line section. It was from here that the fateful moves were made, which sadly set a course for disaster. Lessons are always learned from incidents such as the Weeton crash. For anything of this nature to take place, all the pieces of the jig-saw need to be there. It is only when the last piece drops into place that the inevitable becomes unavoidable.

Pictures by *Roy Anderson* and *Paul Claxton*

Singleton Bank to Singleton

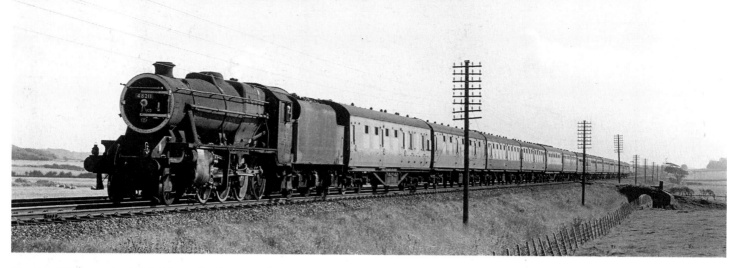

Monday, 27th September 1965. **(Above)** Stanier Class Eight freight engines were well liked for heavy empty stock work. Getting twenty coaches on the move with those little driving wheels was far easier for instance, than with a Black Five or 5X. Many Stanier Black Fives, especially those in the 50 and 51 series, for example 5025 and 5111, would have slipped getting away on Blackpool sands if you let them. A good balanced 8F was a real asset on carriage pilot jobs. Here, **48211** rolls steadily along on the embankment just after the site of Singleton (old) station. The railway here effectively runs parallel to the coast and briefly runs north for a little over three miles. As you took the right hand sweeping curve at Mythop Road bridge (Stanley Hill) and passed the point where the crash was in 1961, the railway then begins this short run north and even on the warmest and sunniest of days you get a strong cross wind entering the cab. Sometimes the breeze is slight and warm but on other occasions it can be wild and a little too bracing. As we look at 48211, the coast, with Blackpool Tower prominent as the tallest landmark is to the right across the open and quite flat landscape almost four miles away. Just to the right of the engine across the first field is a large wood set on slightly higher ground and you can see it from the train all the way from Stanley Hill. It is called Brockholes Wood and to me it looks the same today as it did on my first outing over the North line almost 40 years ago. **(below)** *Clan McCleod*, No. **72008** passes beneath bridge 37 on its way out of Poulton. The view is taken very near to where 48211 is seen, maybe Paul has just walked down the field a little. The Clan had been cleaned by Peter Fitton and Chris Spring on North shed earlier that day and was taking special 1X40 (for Glasgow) back to Carlisle. It was booked to leave the North station at 2 o'clock. You will see 72008 being cleaned on shed in the reprise volume along with others that received voluntary cleaning attention in those final years of steam. Pictures by *Paul Claxton*

POULTON

(above) Crewe based 'Black Fives' **45020** and **45429** ease the Royal Train out of Poulton goods yard. This was the original Preston & Wyre alignment of the railway which took a straight, more direct run through Poulton out to Thornton, en-route to Fleetwood. The curve round towards Blackpool proved to be just a bit too tight as trains grew bigger and faster and a totally new layout was adopted, hence the station we have today, which thankfully has changed little over the years; even the platforms have kept their length. The Royal visit we see here was the last made by the 'old' King, George VI and Queen Elizabeth to the Fylde coast in 1951. Four years later, it was the turn of the young Queen Elizabeth II and Prince Philip to pay a fleeting visit. Ken Bradshaw was on the footplate of the train engine on the journey in on that occasion. He was kitted out with new overalls, cap and badge *et al*, but was asked to hand them back to the stores as he signed off duty. As we see in the picture, to the left side are the avoiding or fast lines, which started here by Poulton No. 1 signalbox and ran parallel with the station platforms through to Poulton No. 3 cabin. You could access the Fleetwood route from them. (below) We are up by the platform end now looking down towards where the 'Black Fives'(above) are standing, adjacent to No. 1 signalbox. The lines seen in this lower picture are the Up Loop, the Up and Down platform lines, the Down the Carriage Loop and on the far right are the avoiding lines. The signalbox is No. 2 cabin.

Splitting at Poulton. Certain trains throughout the day going into the North station also carried a portion of carriages for Fleetwood. It was usually just two or three coaches. **(above)** Fleetwood's **84016** waits patiently for the arrival of 2P64, the 1/40pm from Manchester Victoria. Sure enough at the allotted time, 45256 squeals its way into the very lengthy island platform at Poulton. Little time will be lost easing up and detaching the rear two bogies and once the driver of 45256 has 'blown - up'

again and the guard has rounded everybody up and whistled 'right away', the bulk of the carriages will slip away round the corner towards Carleton Crossing and out of the sidings will steam 84016 to couple up to the small Fleetwood portion and depart at 3/27pm, calling at all stations to Fleetwood. The same procedure though slightly more involved, took place on the other side of the station as portions from Fleetwood were attached to Manchester bound trains and the like. There was a double crossover

on the Up side and the train engine would, after being unhooked, slip forward into the top end of the loop. The 'tanky' with the carriages to attach would run down the loop off the Fleetwood line and slip out onto the Up Main line before reversing onto the main train. It would then uncouple, drop down, go across the road to the Down side and park up. The main train engine could then back up, couple up, then 'blow – up' the brake and make ready to depart. Sounds easy doesn't it ? Pictures by *Paul Claxton* and *Peter Fitton*

POULTON

Those lengthy Poulton platforms. This particular picture always makes me think of Ken Bradshaw. The first time I saw it was just after I had finished working with Ken, and his stories of working the 8.4am businessman's train to Manchester were very fresh in my mind. The 8.4 was the Fleetwood answer to the 'Blackpool Club Trains' which took the business people 'into town' each morning. The platforms at Poulton were very long, you could just squeeze 15 coaches on if need be. The train seen here incidentally, though looking like the 8.4am was in fact a summer working which ran from June through to September to Manchester Victoria and was always booked standing time at Wyre Dock Junction whilst the engine picked up a van load of fish. Up to June 1961, it was coded C351 and thereafter 1J32. It always left Fleetwood at 10.20am, Poulton (10.45 - 47am), before calling at Preston (11.12am), Chorley 11.30am, then on to Bolton, Salford and Manchester. It was nearly always a 'Crab' turn right into the 1960's. The one Ken worked, the 8.4, was C349 until June 1961 when it became 1J18 before ceasing to run in 1964. It called all stations to Poulton, then Preston,

after which it ran non-stop to Salford via Dobbs Brow and Pendlebury, by–passing Bolton and reaching Manchester Victoria at 9.27am. Ken's regular mate at one time on this turn was the genial Hughie Richmond. He was a brilliant engineman who came to Fleetwood from Accrington and was a keen wearer of clogs, often doing an impromptu clog dance on the footplate for Ken. Many a time when Hughie knew young Ken had been out dancing in Blackpool the night before, he would say to Ken *'Ista tired this morning Ken….thee drive an I'll fire today'.* There were always one or two really fussy business characters who boarded the train at Poulton and who always wanted to get into the same part of a carriage every morning. As the 8.4 snaked its way round the tight bend into Poulton's Up platform, Hughie would put a bit of brake in, then walk across the footplate to Ken's side and peering over Ken's shoulder through the front spy glass, he would say *'na..then where's that clever bugger today ?....'* . Ken would eagerly shout, *'there he is, I've got him, he's half down the platform'.* *'Reet',* Hughie would say *'We'll run right well down today, he have to bloody walk'.*

With that, Hughie would cross back over and prepare to stop right down the far end of the platform. Once at a stand, Hughie would dash back across the cab to Ken and looking back together, they would see the chap come running down, waving his fist in the direction of the engine as he hurried aboard amidst the whistling up of the station staff. Jack Crossley was another good mate Ken worked with on the 8.4 passenger. One day when it was Ken's turn to drive, they'd had a bad run to Pendlebury and were late. Even so, Jack was getting peckish and began preparing his partly cooked breakfast on the shovel ready to place it in the fire hole, to quickly cook it as they were creeping up to an adverse signal. Ken was all but at a stand when clunk… off came the signal and Ken went for the regulator and yanked it wide open without thinking…..poor old Jack was just putting his bacon and egg in the fire hole and 'whoosh', there it was….. gone !... No amount of grovelling on Ken's part could ease matters. One thing I can tell you is that it was a quiet ride back on the cushions that day.

Picture by *Alan Gilbert*

Poulton's island platform. (below) The Downside face of the island platform used by trains going into Blackpool or on to Fleetwood is seen the way it looked in the later 1960's when British Railways had given way to being British Rail and staff were being issued with that hideous continental style uniform. I never remember anyone looking smart in that clobber be they footplate or traffic grades. Overall, Poulton station has been very lucky. Just about every other classic station structure around the Fylde has either been unsympathetically modernised or completely destroyed. Now the silly years are over on the railway and the appreciation of quality construction is far greater, lets hope Poulton station with care will be with us for years to come.

On the platform. (Above) It is the 6th August 1958 (Wednesday) and in the Up side platform (far left), is loco **45500** *Patriot* seen down by the signals near Station Road bridge. The train it is pulling is C329, which is the 5.10pm from Blackpool North to Manchester Victoria. This is one of those trains which attached a portion on the front from Fleetwood, in this case at 5/20pm. The train engine is drawing forward so that the coaches from Fleetwood can come off the branch and along the Up Loop before being crossed into the Up side platform so that they can then be shunted back onto the Manchester bound train ready for departure at 5/26pm. Now then, looking on the platform where the station lamp is visible, look just to the left of it. There in the far distance underneath the bridge, down by the No. 2 signalbox is tank engine **84018,** which is sitting in the neck end of the Downside carriage road. The engine is awaiting the arrival of the 4/55pm Manchester Victoria to Blackpool North train, which will depart Poulton leaving the rear portion for Fleetwood, which 84018 will take forward at 6/5pm. Lastly, nearest the camera, is tank engine **41261** and two coaches. They are waiting the arrival of the 4/10pm from Manchester (C344), which should appear at 5/37pm and with the Fleetwood portion detached and the main train having departed to Blackpool, 41261 will back up and leave for Fleetwood at 5/42pm, all being well.

The three views here are as follows. On the right we are looking along the Downside platform towards the overbridge at Breck Road. The lines on the left are the avoiding lines. These fast lines merged with the slow lines just beyond the bridge by the No. 3 signalbox as we can see in the picture below. Trains to and from Fleetwood could also use them. The trackwork by Poulton No. 3, as we can see, was quite complex. **(below right)** Here is the station entrance on the bridge at Breck Road.

Parting of the ways. 45256, which we saw arriving at Poulton on page 36, is now getting under way on the last leg of its journey to Blackpool North, at 3/22pm on Saturday the 29th August 1964. It will call at Layton at 3/26pm and be at the buffers in North station by 3/30pm. The train was coded C252 until June 1961, thereafter it became 2P64. You can see the all important fast lines curving away to the right beneath the second and third coaches. The station buildings on the bridge at Breck Road are visible and the platforms are down below them. **(below)** Just five minutes after 45256 had gone by, little 'tanky' **84016** steams off towards Thornton to call all stations to Fleetwood, where it should arrive at 3/42pm. Pictures by *Paul Claxton* and *Peter Fitton*

By Poulton No. 3

(Above) On Saturday 13th August 1966, 'Black Five' **45197** was working the 'Dundee' out of Blackpool North and the driver has eased down for the 35mph speed restriction covering the section of line which began at Poulton No. 4 signal box. The 35mph continues round the fast lines, 45197 being routed that way. The slow lines via the platforms are only 20mph. The 'Dundee' really will not 'get crackin' till he gets towards bridge 37 on the run out to Singleton. Then, the fireman will have to set to and 'get stuck in' for the run to Preston.

(right) Quietly does it, as **60022** *Mallard* eases across onto the Down line using the crossover in the picture above (by 45197). This famous engine was visiting Blackpool with the Northern Rubber Company outing to the ' lights' had just completed turning on the Poulton triangle, turning the observation car at the same time. Now they are on their way back to Enfield Road carriage sidings.

Pictures by *Frank Dean*

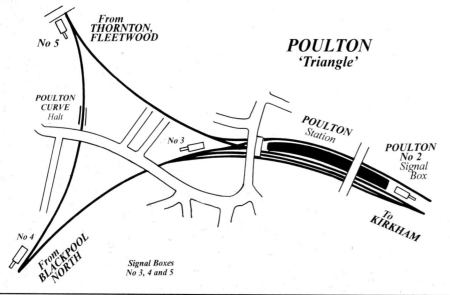

On the last leg. Leaving Poulton, as I found out in the later 1960's, when I first started going to Blackpool North, you get that feeling as you snake your way round the wide sweeping bend leading to Carleton that.... Yes you are getting very close to journeys end. Maybe it's the bright light from the coast or the style of housing and construction. From hereon in through Carleton Crossing round to Layton, the Tower is there in the distance growing ever nearer now and you feel by Layton that you really are in the suburbs, just the way you do entering London when you see the back sides of all those 'yellowy' brick terraces around Camden. **(above) 44730** brings the 1/50pm to Manchester into Poulton beneath the bridge carrying Tithebarn Street on Thursday 23rd July 1964. Picture by *Peter Fitton*

CARLETON CROSSING TO LAYTON

Carleton Crossing. As you left the wide sweeping curve at Poulton No. 4 signalbox, where the Fleetwood line took off to go round the curve towards Poulton Curve Halt, the line ran along in a straight formation the short distance to Carleton Crossing, rising quite steadily as it did so. **D73** (above), is just levelling off at the top of that rise by the signalbox there. The train it is covering is the 4/3pm from Manchester to Blackpool North on the 11th May 1963. Carleton Crossing is again a name I can't bring to mind without hearing Ken Bradshaw's pronunciation in my head. I can see him now, he is sat there, legs crossed, pipe in mouth and playing with his lighter in one hand as he makes a valid point with the other. Leaving Carleton, Blackpool Tower is now prominent on the skyline. The line edges left again past Higher Moor Farm bridge and drops down into Layton beneath Plymouth Road bridge, where (left) we see *Mallard* passing in September 1961. Pictures by

Peter Fitton and **Tony Bretherton**

Layton station. Blackpool North station is only now about a mile away. As Layton was passed, the style of high grade red brick housing and the bustle of traffic, not to mention the odd cream and green coloured double decker bus, really did tell you it was time to start gathering your things together for the run into the North station was about to begin in earnest.

Layton, a little 'gem'. I do have a soft spot for Layton. Certain stations do appeal greatly, St.Annes was another. **(above)** The lovely little waiting room on the Downside (going in) is thought to have come from Deepdale near Preston. **(below)** The station is seen from the slope leading to Plymouth Road bridge. We are looking in the Blackpool direction and the main buildings are visible on the Up side. Over on **page 45 (top)** is a view from the footbridge taken on the 15th September 1962 at 3/21pm. One of Gorton shed's many 'Crab' 2-6-0's No. **42748**, slips by the station, the coaches no doubt echoing a bit as they pass beneath the ornate concrete bridge at Plymouth Road. 1T05 was a trip to the 'lights' from Hadfield. At the bottom on page 45 are the Up side buildings, outside which is a station seat (of L&Y origin) by the luggage office. Ken Bradshaw and his mate Tommy Stanhope, when working the last train to Fleetwood out of the North station one night, had trouble with a drunk who was quite incapable, so they each grabbed an arm and a leg and bundled him into a compartment on the old push and pull train and knowing he always alighted normally at Layton they decided to see that he got there. Having arrived at Layton, Ken and Tommy both grabbed hold of the man and hoisted him out and across onto the bench seat we mentioned at the beginning by the luggage offices. Here they laid him out to sleep it off. One dark night, Ken was on the engine at the rear, pushing hard near Layton when the two carriages jumped and rolled wildly. It seems that kids had placed big stones on the line trying to derail the train …. And almost did !....... Picture of 42748 by *Peter Fitton*

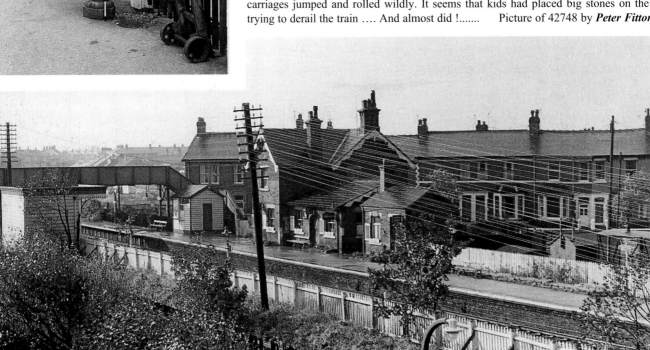

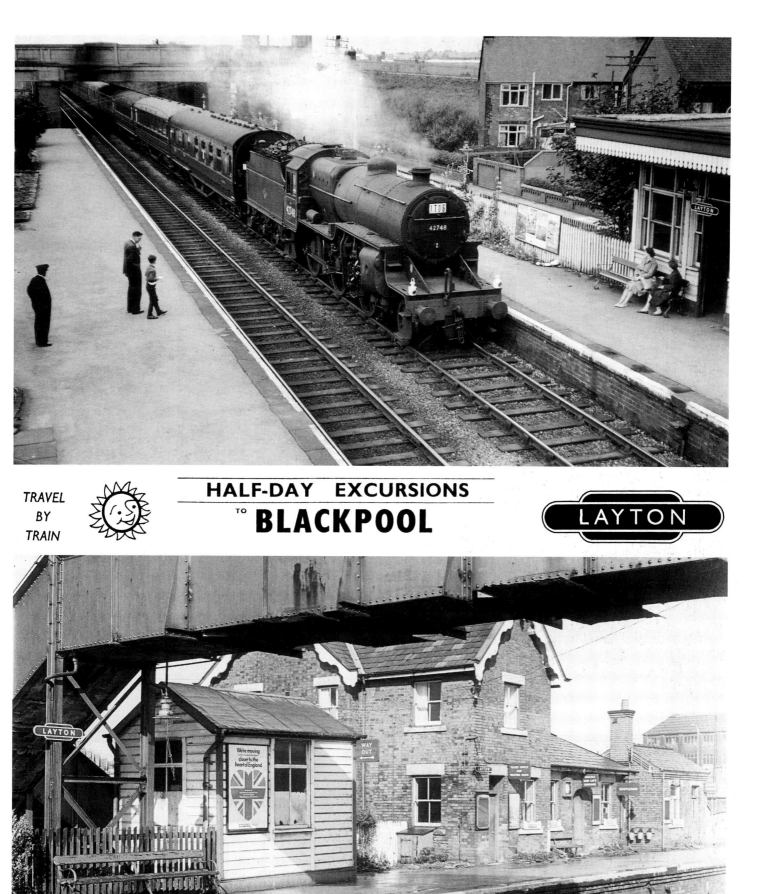

TRAVEL BY TRAIN

HALF-DAY EXCURSIONS TO **BLACKPOOL**

LAYTON

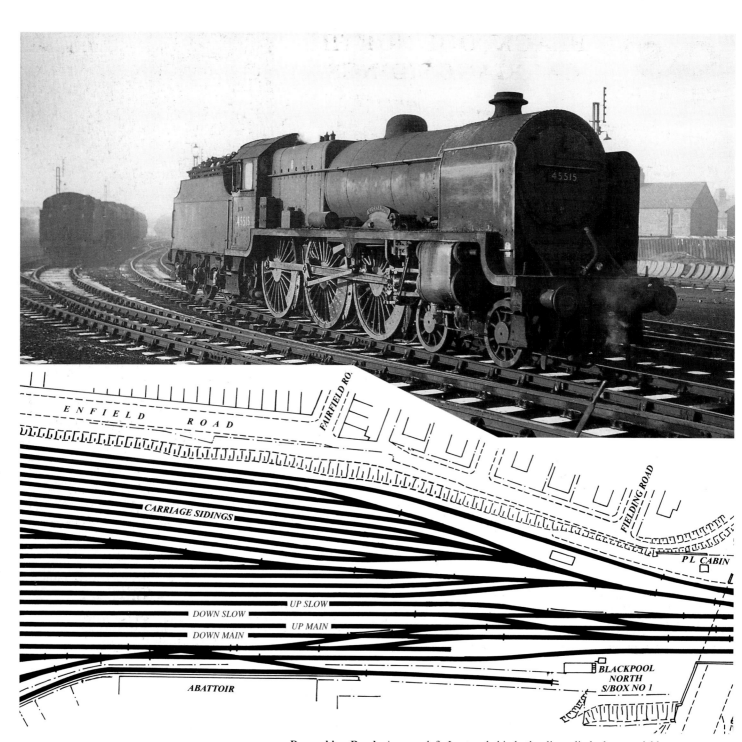

Devonshire Road. As you left Layton behind, the line climbed appreciably to pass over Devonshire Road bridge. The bridge here carried the railway above the B5124, a minor but nevertheless busy road that ran between Bispham and Whitegate Drive, joining the main A583 at that point. As you climbed to the bridge looking out on the right side, you would see the headshunt of the carriage sidings next to Enfield Road. Across on the left side of the line, if you had the window down, then the lovely smell of warm biscuits baking would waft into the carriage from the nearby Symbol biscuits factory. On those odd outings in the later 1960's with mum and dad, mum was always quick to comment how good it was that the biscuit works was still with us. Nearly another 40 years on they are still making biscuits there and the smell is just as good today as it ever was. As you may recall from the other volumes, mum was a connoisseur of all things sweet and crumbly. As you journeyed ever nearer towards the North station there was also the lingering smell of Catterall and Swarbricks famous Blackpool brewery always well known for its traditional dark beers. The brewery was over to the left not too far from the railway. The picture on the right **(page 47)** shows **45684** *Jutland* leaving the resort and passing over Devonshire Road bridge on the 4th August 1965 with a train for Liverpool Exchange. The main signals on the bracket arms protect the Down Main line and the Down Slow line. The latter allowed you to run into the excursion station without holding up the passage of trains in and out of the main station.

X-L ALE

Class 6P5F 4-6-0 No. 45623 Palestine [Eric Treacy]

Class 6P5F 4-6-0 No. 45518 Bradshaw [Brian E. Morrison]

Class 8P 4-6-2 No. 46205 Princess Victoria (with inside valve gear operated by rocking shafts) [T. K. Widd]

Class 5MT 4-6-0 No. 45298 (with self-weighing tender) [J. B. Bucknall]

Class 5MT 4-6-0 No. 45480 (with top feed on front boiler ring) [P. H. Groom]

Class 6P5F 4-6-0 No. 45524 Blackpool [J. R. Carter]

'Patriots' at Blackpool

It is Boxing day in 1961 and whilst most of us were sitting round a cosy fire probably enjoying the benefit of one of the first Christmases when we had a television, young Paul Claxton braved the cold freezing air lingering around the shed yard at Blackpool North to film Patriot engine **45515** *Caernarvon* (left - page 46) , as it shunted about by the 'winterised' engines that were an annual sight in the winter months for many years here at the North shed. In the Ian Allan ABC above two Patriots are seen 45518 *Bradshaw* (no, not named after Ken) and 45524 Blackpool.   **Paul Claxton**

To
KIRKHAM, FLEETWOOD
PRESTON

BRIDGE
(No 122)

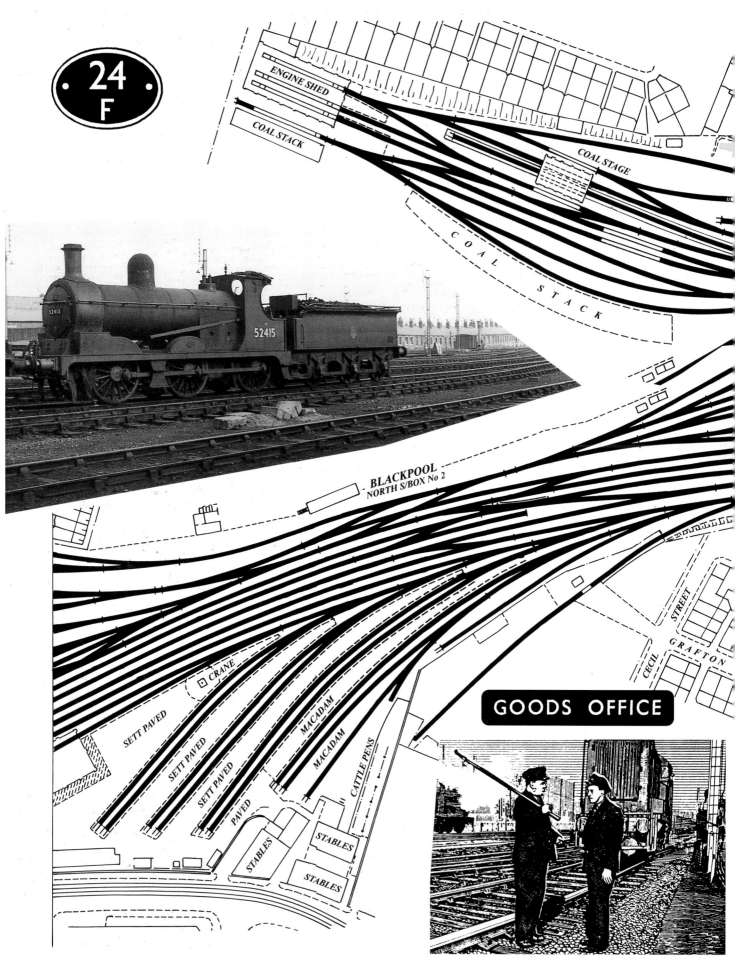

24
F

ENGINE SHED

COAL STACK

COAL STAGE

C O A L   S T A C K

52415

BLACKPOOL
NORTH S/BOX No 2

CRANE

SETT PAVED

SETT PAVED

SETT PAVED

PAVED

MACADAM

MACADAM

CATTLE PENS

STABLES

STABLES

STABLES

STREET

GRAFTON

CECIL

GOODS OFFICE

BLACKPOOL NORTH

Blackpool North station and sidings covered a wide area and dealt with large numbers of holidaymakers every year up until about 1967. By then the winding down process was well advanced and road traffic was increasing rapidly. Most of the changes and rationalisation of the lines seen here would occur in the early 1970s.

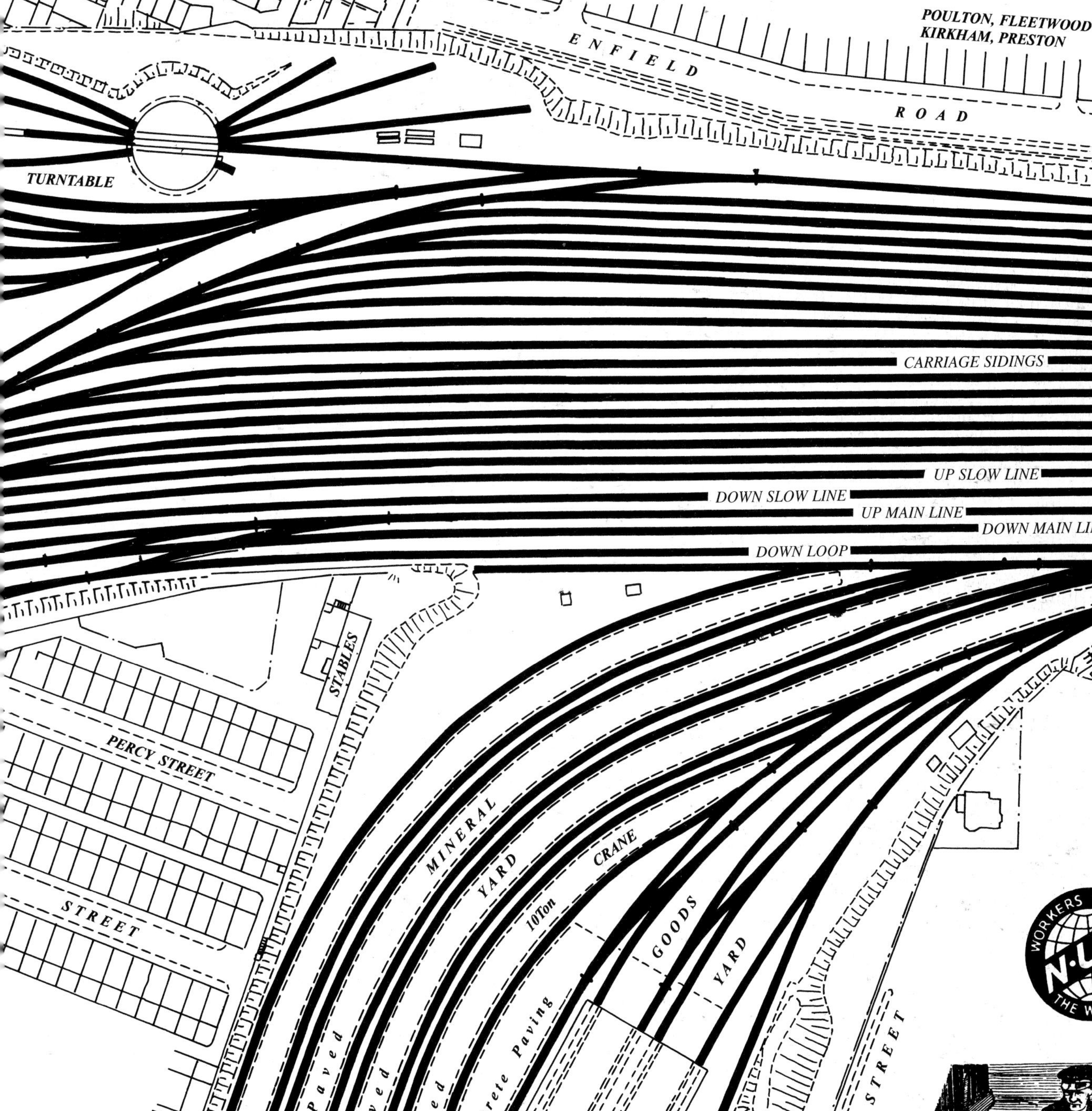

POULTON, FLEETWOOD
KIRKHAM, PRESTON

E N F I E L D   R O A D

TURNTABLE

CARRIAGE SIDINGS

UP SLOW LINE

DOWN SLOW LINE

UP MAIN LINE

DOWN MAIN LINE

DOWN LOOP

STABLES

PERCY STREET

STREET

MINERAL

YARD

10Ton CRANE

GOODS

YARD

Sett Paved

Sett Paved

Sett Paved

Concrete Paving

GOODS

GOODS SHED

GOODS OFFICES

ROAD MOTOR WORKSHOPS

ABATTOIR STREET

WORKERS OF THE WORLD UNITE
N·U·R

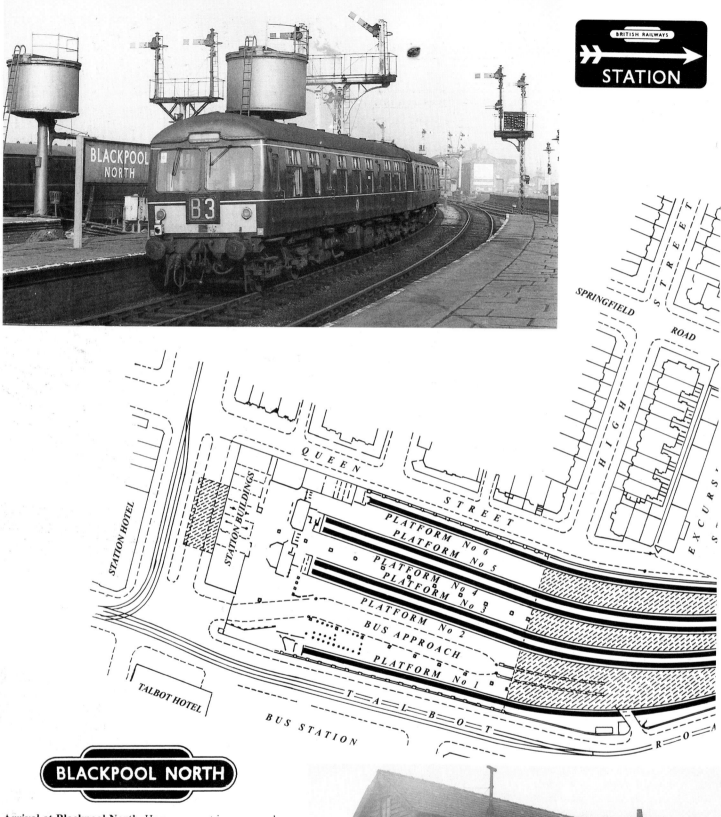

SPRINGFIELD ROAD

STREET

HIGH

EXCURSION

STATION HOTEL

STATION BUILDINGS

QUEEN STREET

PLATFORM No 6
PLATFORM No 5
PLATFORM No 4
PLATFORM No 3
PLATFORM No 2
BUS APPROACH
PLATFORM No 1

TALBOT HOTEL

BUS STATION

TALBOT ROAD

BLACKPOOL NORTH

Arrival at Blackpool North. Here we are at journeys end, at Blackpool North. As you snaked your way down into the main station, you seemed to be enveloped by the high blue brick walls and the semi darkness beneath the overall roof. It was very similar in many ways to the Woodside terminus at Birkenhead. No. 3 signal box (seen to the right) was situated by the loading dock. The signalman here controlled all movements within the station platforms, numbers one to six. The top picture shows a Cravens set (DMU) leaving platform three for Fleetwood. Picture by *Peter Fitton*

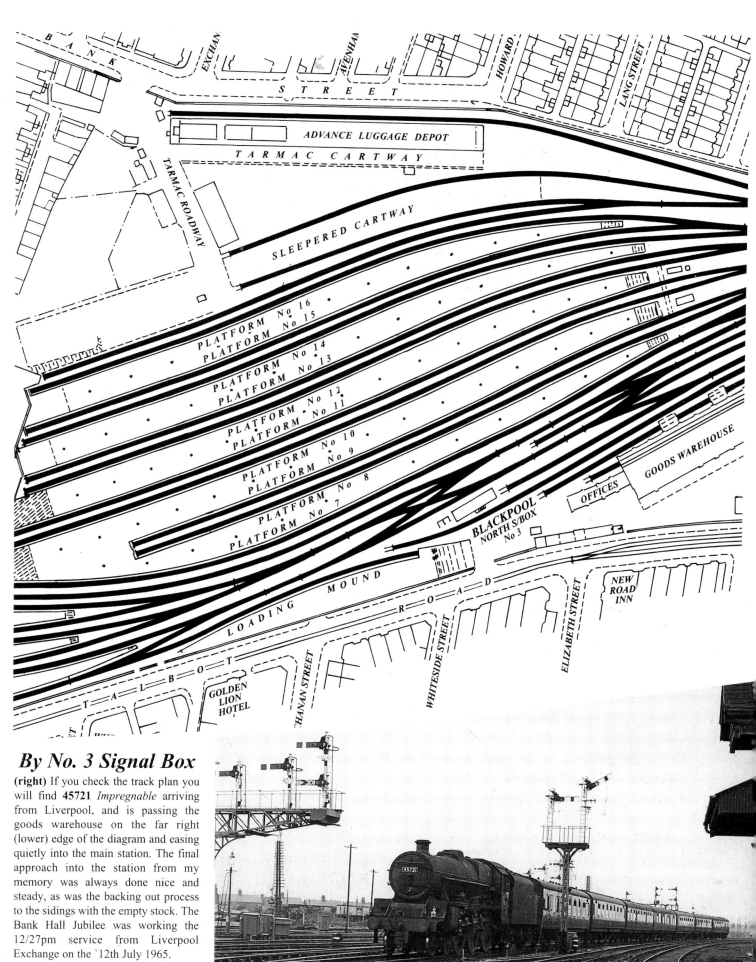

BANK

EXCHANGE

STREET

AVENHAM

HOWARD

LANG STREET

ADVANCE LUGGAGE DEPOT

TARMAC CARTWAY

TARMAC ROADWAY

SLEEPERED CARTWAY

PLATFORM No 16
PLATFORM No 15
PLATFORM No 14
PLATFORM No 13
PLATFORM No 12
PLATFORM No 11
PLATFORM No 10
PLATFORM No 9
PLATFORM No 8
PLATFORM No 7

GOODS WAREHOUSE

OFFICES

BLACKPOOL
NORTH S/BOX
No 3

LOADING MOUND

NEW
ROAD
INN

ROAD

WHITESIDE STREET

ELIZABETH STREET

BUCHANAN STREET

TALBOT

GOLDEN
LION
HOTEL

By No. 3 Signal Box

(right) If you check the track plan you will find **45721** *Impregnable* arriving from Liverpool, and is passing the goods warehouse on the far right (lower) edge of the diagram and easing quietly into the main station. The final approach into the station from my memory was always done nice and steady, as was the backing out process to the sidings with the empty stock. The Bank Hall Jubilee was working the 12/27pm service from Liverpool Exchange on the `12th July 1965.

Picture by *Peter Fitton*

51

Entering Blackpool North. It was a very gentle approach into the platforms here at the North station. The speed was well down, probably 15mph by the warehouse, dropping to 10mph by No. 3 signal box as the platform end came near. This slow approach into the station gave you ample time to take every thing in. The huge blue/brown tinged coping stones which lined the platform edges at the North were very memorable with their distinctive bevelled edge. As you descended into the train shed, high above you was the blue brick wall bordering the top end of Talbot Road. The hustle and bustle of passing traffic was all apparent. There was the smell of stale beer in the air from the pubs up on Talbot Road and the sun would be shining brightly and the Tower seemed unbelievably close. The noise of busy Blackpool was all around you. Once you slipped inside the confines of the train shed much of the surrounding noise gave way to the squeal of wheels binding against the rails and the hiss of steam or even the lifting of safety valves as the train engine clanked its way towards the buffers. **45721** is again seen running into the North station with the 12/27pm from Liverpool Exchange (1P67). It is not however the same day as the earlier view on page 51 even though it is the same engine and even the same coaching stock. Little differences in the appearance of the engine give that away. Over on the left a set of men are seen making their way across to the platform, no doubt to relieve the Bank Hall men so they can get their grub. The Ramsden Arms hotel seen behind the wall in the top right of the picture was a favourite liquid lunch spot for loco crews. You could reach it quickly by nipping across to the loading dock and out onto Talbot Road.

Blackpool

THE BEST ON THE COAST

On this page, the smaller picture (bottom left) shows the old 'Lanky' heating boiler on its siding between the 'two' stations. In this volume we only deal with the main station and platforms numbers one to six, as these are the only platforms I recall from our earlier excursion years. Never fear, the excursion platforms are seen in detail as well as the main station in the final volume - still to come - that looks at the end of the excursion era in the years up to 1967. The large picture here on page 53 is the view of platforms No's 1-6 as seen from the siding by the heating boiler. Pictures *Paul Claxton* and *Stuart Taylor*.

BLACKPOOL NORTH

Buffering up. Tank engine No. 42460 shuffles into platform two and onto the rear of the stock of the 12/27pm from Liverpool Exchange. As mentioned earlier, engine crews arriving at the seaside generally had a thirst to quench and the three pubs by the station on Talbot Road proved very handy, especially if you were getting relieved and going home 'on the cushions'. In the far left of the picture looking along the wall side, you can see the gateway off the loading dock out onto the top end of Talbot Road, which conveniently led to the Ramsden Arms Hotel (seen above the tank engine). The Wheatsheaf Hotel is the modern pub seen above the men on the platform. It was always rough and ready and not as well liked by enginemen; maybe the landlord didn't look after the ale that well. The third pub was the Kings Arms which really wasn't just handy enough for locomen or was it a little too near the station offices for comfort. The men here having a 'conflab' are in the course of making their way forward to relieve the crew of 45721, but they seem to be hanging back, possibly to arrange with the shunter and pilot engine crew whats to take place in the shunt move. **(below)** On page 55 and looking the other way towards the train shed, little Stanier tank engine No. **40174** is standing in platform two on the 6th August 1958. As you can see, it wasn't easy trying to take pictures here within the confines of the North station. The light was nearly always wrong, but thankfully as cameras progressed in quality and ability, light factors were overcome as we will see to great effect in the reprise volume (26, part 6). Pictures by *Paul Claxton* and *Stuart Taylor*

BLACKPOOL
NORTH

600
BRITISH RAILWAYS (M)
BLACKPOOL (NORTH)
PLATFORM TICKET 1D.
Available One Hour on Day of Issue only
Not Valid in Trains   Not Transferable
To be given up when leaving Platform
(see U)
FOR CONDITIONS SEE OVER
1 | 2 | 3 | 4 | 5 | 6
7 | 8 | 9 | 10 | 11 | 12
600

BLACKPOOL (NORTH).

Setting back of empty trains from station (Nos. 1 to 6 platforms) to carriage sidings:—

The rear Guards of trains arriving at Blackpool (North) must stand in sight of the shunt-back signals, so as to be able to call the Drivers back (with green hand signal) directly the signals are taken off. Driver (and front Guard if there be any) must be on the alert to obey such signals immediately.

Repeating signals—Nos. 1 to 6 Platform Roads:—

Unless instructions to the contrary are given by the Station Master, engines detached at the buffers must follow the departing train out at a safe distance to the platform starting signal, but must not pass that signal until it has been placed to Danger and again taken off.

When a train arrives double-headed the engines must remain coupled together unless the Station Master gives instructions to the contrary.

During the time No. 2 box is closed no movement must take place from the carriage sidings at that box in the direction of the station or to and from Bank Street Sidings, Nos. 14, 15 and 16 roads, until permission has been obtained, by telephone, from the Signalman at No. 3 box, and the latter must be advised immediately the movement is again clear of the engine shed running line. The Signalman at No. 3 box must also be advised immediately movements to these sidings are clear of the engine shed running line.

End of the first train trip

This for the moment is journey's end. Now we are going out on the streets of Blackpool to look at the years from the 1950's to 1962. We will be looking at scenes around the Central and North pier areas where the main entertainment could be found. Having a look at the stars who performed twice nightly at the resorts top venues, we can follow the changes from the almost music hall era to the very 'with it' days of the 1960's when modern music and pop groups took over. You will have noticed that I didn't attempt to personalise the run from Kirkham to the North station in the way that I have previously done in the other outings in the series. The reason is because we, as a complete family, never did travel over this route. We only ever used the North station in the 1950's and up to 1964 to travel out to Fleetwood and always on the last day of the Runabout day rover. Having arrived early on the Friday we would make our way up to the North station via Abingdon Street Market. After a steady look around the market stalls and a quick lunch break, it was off to the North station to catch the little shuttle service to

Fleetwood for the famous Friday market. I therefore have two very different memories of the North station. One as a youngster dashing into the caverness train shed excited at the Friday outing, always considered a real treat. The second was of the later years (1966-68)' by which time I was at work and the railways were a daily part of life. Ale houses, dodgy mess rooms and a railway system that was disappearing before our very eyes all quickly dispelled the notions of my happy family outings. I won't dwell here on those feelings, they will come out in due course in the reprise volume and you can make your own judgements on the era. **(above)** This is the concourse just the way I remember it near the refreshment rooms and platforms five and six. **On page 57** at the top is the taxi road between platforms No's. one and two. **Below left** are mum and dad, you will have seen it before but I had to include it. Dad's grey suit did sterling service over the years and mum….well she was always happiest perusing the book stalls looking at the magazines, when we had time to kill. Those books of the stars were her favourites. Another one turned up recently. It was volume two from 1960 and had Marty Wilde on the front cover.

TOP NUMBERS' **BOOK OF THE STARS**

No. 10

TOP NUMBERS' **BOOK OF THE STARS**

RICHARD CHAMBERLAIN

TOP NUMBERS' **BOOK OF THE STARS**

No. 13 Price 2/6 d. CLIFF RICHARD

TOP NUMBERS' **BOOK OF THE STARS**

No. 9 BILLY FURY

57

In the next few pages, we are going to span the years of entertainment in the resort. We will be looking at how things appeared post war/early 1950's, then follow them right through to the early 1960's. By 1962, the big names of stage and television had to take a back seat as youth culture (horrible modern term) took over in the shape of pop stars like Cliff and the Shadows, Billy Fury, Marty Wilde and Joe Brown. By 1962 the traditional older stars of stage and the music hall era were fading fast. It was the end of yet another era, never again would we see the wealth of stars or the variety of acts all within one resort, so those of you who were there and did see them consider yourselves very lucky indeed.

IMPERIAL DICKSON ROAD
Telephone 20270
TO-DAY (WED.) 2-15, 6-0 Cont.
Last Complete Performance 8-5
Dean Martin   Jerry Lewis
THREE-RING CIRCUS
(U) — Colour by Technicolor
THURS.: WHISPERING SMITH (A)

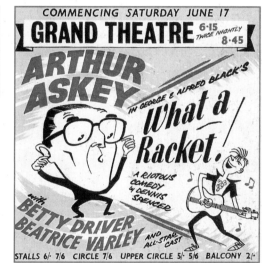

COMMENCING SATURDAY JUNE 17
GRAND THEATRE 6-15 TWICE NIGHTLY 8-45
IN GEORGE & ALFRED BLACK'S
ARTHUR ASKEY
What a Racket!
A RIOTOUS COMEDY by DENNIS SPENCER
with **BETTY DRIVER**
BEATRICE VARLEY AND ALL-STAR CAST
STALLS 6/- 7/6   CIRCLE 7/6   UPPER CIRCLE 5/- 5/6   BALCONY 2/-

CENTRAL PIER ★ BLACKPOOL

COMMENCING 23rd MAY, 1958

Twice Nightly, 6.00 and 8.30.   Matinee Thursday, 2.30
Prices 6/- and 4/6
★ ★ ★ ★
"LET'S HAVE FUN"
WITH THE
KEN DODD SHOW
starring
KEN DODD, DON LANG (from B.B.C. 6.5 Special)
Also Guest Star JOSEF LOCKE
AND A FULL CAST OF STAR ARTISTES

Stars galore. Here we see famous faces of the early 1950's who remained popular right through the decade. **(left)** The Mudlarks look surprised at their success. Their 'Lollipop' hit record of the summer of 1958 really was catchy with old and young alike. Over on page 61 at the top is Ruby Murray, a firm favourite at Blackpool all through the 1950's and the 1960's as well. Joan Regan, elegant as ever, played the Queen's in 1955. Pearl Carr and Teddy Johnson, aided by Pet Clarke performed at the North Pier for Bernard Delfont in the later 1950s. Eve Boswell, the South African beauty is seen getting ready for a performance at the Palace Theatre. Finally, two of the top names of the mid 1950's were Edna Savage and Terry Dene. I have put them together because they were briefly married. Edna from Warrington became a radio star in 1954 in Manchester and just two years later she topped the bill at the Blackpool Palace Theatre in the 'Summer Showboat' with Mike and Bernie Winters. Hit records followed, often competing for chart positions with Joan Savage (no relation) and Ruby Murray. Listening to her now still sends a shiver through you. Her voice was like velvet, quite haunting in many ways. Terry Dene *(A White, Sports Coat, and a Pink carnation* - remember it *?)* was very different in style and manner. She met him whilst playing summer season at the Winter Gardens in Morecambe in 1957. Alma Cogan was also on the bill. They married in 1958 when Terry's career was at its height, the pressures were many. It was just too much for two young people, such as they were, to cope with.

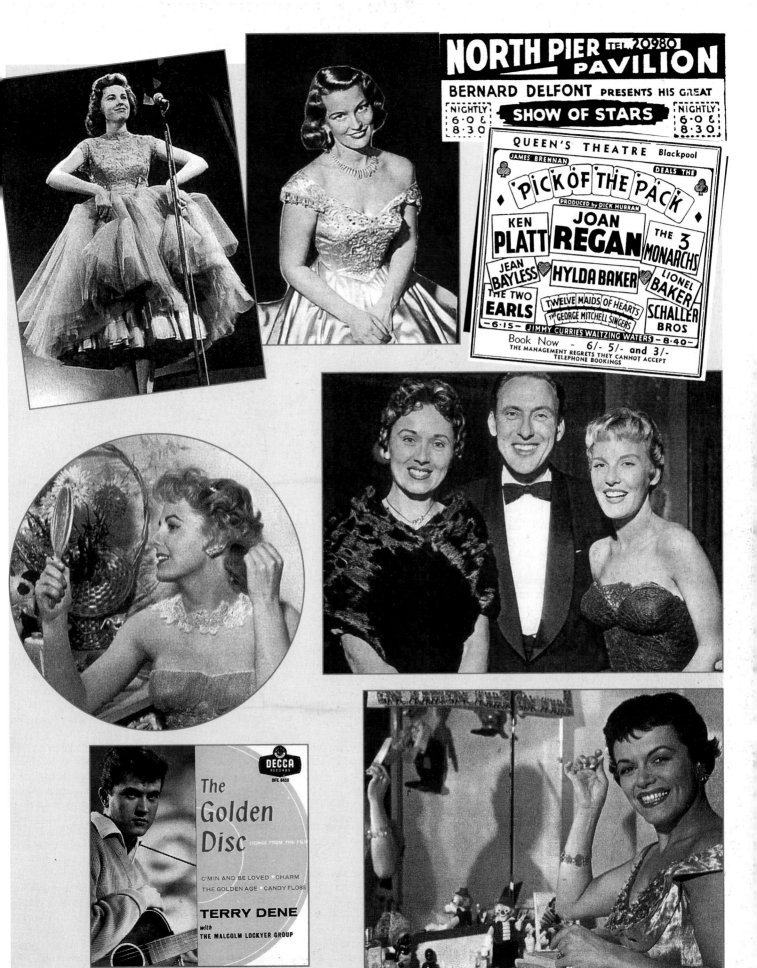

DECCA
RECORDS
DFE 6459

The
**Golden
Disc**
(SONGS FROM THE FILM)

C'MIN AND BE LOVED · CHARM
THE GOLDEN AGE · CANDY FLOSS

TERRY DENE
with
THE MALCOLM LOCKYER GROUP

Goodbye......we wish you all a last good bye !..........In the immediate post war years and through the 1950's, many traditional stars of radio and cinema would be seen year after year at Blackpool. Sadly, all this would change with the onset of the 1960's. The older stars of the war years began to fade quite quickly. Like other things in life, changes in show business came indecently fast. Singing sensation Josef Locke serenaded countless thousands at the seaside. He is seen here at the Central Station about to leave the resort with comedian Tommy Trinder whose catchphrase was *'You lucky people'*. Jo Locke played 19 sell out seasons at the resort from 1939 to 1958 and at the end of that final season he did a 'runner' to evade the taxman. He owed £10,500 in back tax. As police closed in to arrest him he was already in hiding in the Irish Republic. He had flown from Squires Gate airport to visit a bloodstock sale. Always keen on the horses, he would turn up at Whitesides farm on the Fylde where Ken Bradshaw's brother Sid worked. Sid, always referred to as 'our kid' by Ken, recalled that Jo Locke would treat the lads to an impromptu concert in the farmyard getting them to join in with choruses of his most popular tunes. Back in 1950, he was earning £1000 a week and a tour of the states netted him £100,000 in the mid 1950's. As an impresario, he hired a young Julie Andrews for Four Guineas a week and signed Morecambe and wise for £35 a week. He eventually some years later surfaced, paid off his debts and found fame again in his twilight years. George Formby continued to play locally during the season in the 1950's, despite failing health and continuing problems at home. His last season was in 1960 at the Queens Theatre starring with Yana, the little girl with the large 'buffers'. Blackpool's own Norma Sykes, better known as Sabrina, was even more endowed in the buffer department. She is seen across on page 63 with 'big hearted' Arthur Askey who was another legend of the war years and the 1950's. No doubt seeing the busty Sabrina there at such close quarters to him, the words of one of his catchphrases must be foremost in his mind as he smiles for the camera *'before your very eyes' !*...

David Whitfield. Without a doubt the top British singing voice of the 1950's belonged to David Whitfield, a singer who instilled passion into every song and whose voice was quite exceptional. He was a former seaman from Hull, who was working in a cement works when fame came knocking. By the middle of the decade he had amassed a huge catalogue of hits and album tracks. In those heady days of the 1950's his records quite often stayed in the charts for months on end, 20 to 30 weeks being normal. *Answer Me, Cara Mia* and *My September Love* are amongst the best remembered of his records. The last one mentioned repeatedly entered the pop charts in 1956 in the spring, summer, and autumn of 1956. I remember well the awnings outside of the Opera House where a larger than life David Whitfield was looking down on Church Street that summer of 1958. Mum was mad on him and I can see her now on the Friday dinner time that year taking a breather before heading along to the Market in Abingdon Street resting one hand on her hip and staring across at David Whitfield's picture, seemingly in a trance till dad shouted, *'C'mon Daisy lets be going'*.....

Church Street, Blackpool. Blackpool's main street of entertainment was Church Street, you had the Grand Theatre near the bottom, the Winter Gardens and Opera House complex came next. Further up you had the Hippodrome Theatre which was later transformed in to the ABC Theatre and the elegantly proportioned Regent Cinema was right at the top. **(above)** Eddie Calvert sings whilst Ruby Murray plays Eddie's golden trumpet.   **(below)** Dickie Valentine wows the audience at the Hippodrome in 1955.

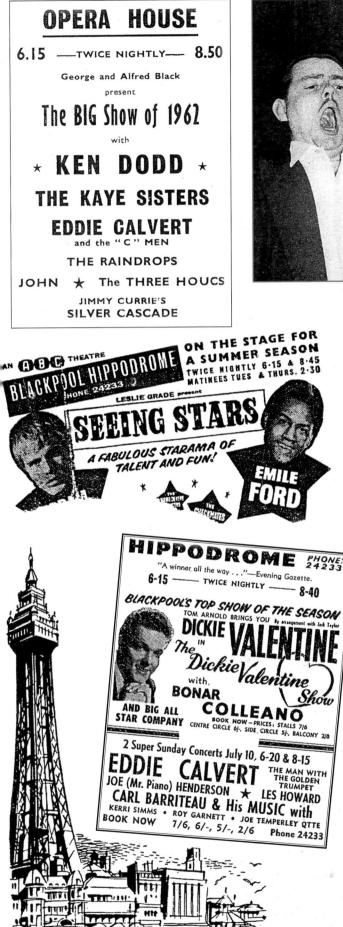

BLACKPOOL'S OTHER Big Shows FOR YOUR ENTERTAINMENT AND ENJOYMENT
★ ★ ★ ★ ★

TOWER BALLROOM
DANCING EACH AFTERNOON
TOMMY JONES and the Tower Band

NIGHTLY from 7-0
to the Music of
REGINALD DIXON
at the Wurlitzer (Tonight excepted)
TOMMY JONES   WATSON HOLMES
and the Tower Band   at the Wurlitzer

General Admission 3/-. Children 1/6

WINTER GARDENS
RESTAURANTS
Fully Licensed ★ Open Daily (Sun. ex.)
LUNCHEONS ★ TEAS
DINNERS
SPECIAL 3-COURSE
LUNCHEON 5/-

PALACE BALLROOM
OLD TIME DANCING NIGHTLY
From 7-0 ★ Admission 2/6
KEN   ★   WATSON
TURNER   HOLMES
and his Orchestra   at the Wurlitzer

PALACE THEATRE
EACH AFTERNOON at 2-30 (Sun. excepted)
COMM. THURS. NEXT for a limited Season
Harold Fielding presents
JACKIE RAE
from "SPOT THE TUNE"
with his famous MUSI-QUIZ

£25 JACKPOT DAILY   HUNDREDS OF POUNDS in other Prizes

BLACKPOOL
1961 / 62

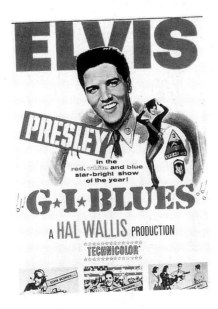

ELVIS
PRESLEY
in the red, white and blue star-bright show of the year!
G·I·BLUES
A HAL WALLIS PRODUCTION
TECHNICOLOR

The best years of entertainment. An abundance of stars appeared at Blackpool in the years from 1955-60. Even Morecambe just up the road boasted a wealth of talent in those prime years of seaside summer shows. One of the big reasons for the upsurge in talent during the season was that so many entertainers were now coming into our own homes via the new medium of television. As the 1950's drew to a close more and more people became 'telly' addicts. We got ours in December 1960, just in time to see the start of Coronation Street. Having seen these artists 'on the box', it seemed only right to see them in person when you were on your holidays. As well as the traditional stage names we suddenly had a host of 'telly' personalities added to this, the new stars in the music world and you had a wide variety of acts to choose from, many to be seen on the same bill. In those heady years at Blackpool, the following stars, and more, could be seen. George Formby, Josef Locke, Tommy Trinder, Arthur Askey, Glenn Melvyn, Thora Hird, Betty Driver, Danny Ross, Jewel and Warriss, Anne Shelton, Joan Regan, Alma Cogan, Eve Boswell, Ruby Murray, Joan Savage, Edna Savage, Frankie Vaughan, Mike and Bernie Winters, Roy Castle, Marion Ryan, Charlie Chester, Morecambe and Wise, Eddie Calvert, Tommy Steele, Adam Faith, Bob Monkhouse and countless others. (below) We see Alma Cogan in conversation with Blackpool's own Gary Miller. Gary played briefly as a junior for Blackpool Football Club, but soon headed for London in search of a singing career. His debut performance took place at the 20th Century Theatre on the same bill as two young hopefuls also treading the boards for the first time, they were Bob Monkhouse and Benny Hill. In the 1960's, Gary, along with Don Spencer, provided a number of the title songs for the early Gerry Anderson puppet programmes.

Stars in town. The best years for stars peaked in 1960 with 1961 seeing a slight down trend where 'pop music' stars began to replace more traditional artists of stage at the top of the bill. This trend continued a pace in the next couple of years and following the emergence of the Merseybeat 'sound' things just never again returned to the overall variety act scene of a few years earlier. In 1960, Tommy Steele, Alma Cogan and Eddie Calvert were at the Opera House, Bob Monkhouse was next door at the Winter Gardens. Danny Ross and Glenn Melvyn were at the Grand Theatre. Ruby Murray and Harry Secombe were at the Palace Theatre, whilst the Hippodrome saw its last years out before refurbishment playing host to the stars of television. The summer shows here were filmed for viewing on the 'telly', being screened on Saturday or Sunday evenings at prime times. 1961 saw the closure of the Palace Theatre and subsequent demolition. Frankie Vaughan topped the bill that final year. Lonnie Donegan was at the Winter Gardens. Arthur Askey was back at the Grand Theatre with Betty Driver. Summer Sunday shows of stars at the Opera House (changing weekly), had Alma Cogan, Joe (Mr Piano) Henderson, Connie Francis, Eddie Calvert, Ronnie Hilton, Adam Faith, Marion Ryan and Mark Wynter. **(right)** It was in the 1962 season that singing sensations Nina and Frederick appeared at the Queen's Theatre. They were seen on page 67 by the theatre entrance and here we see them making friends with the donkeys by the New Inn in Bank Hey Street, with the Central Station just in the background.

BLACKPOOL CENTRAL

8·50 NIGHTLY

6·15 TWICE

OPERA HOUSE
COMMENCING SAT. JULY 1st

GEORGE & ALFRED BLACK present
THE GREATEST SHOW in TOWN!

FROM AUGUST 28th ONWARDS
CLIFF
RICHARD
AND THE SHADOWS

FROM JULY 1st TO AUGUST 26th
AND FOR THE ENTIRE SEASON
THE PERSONAL
APPEARANCE OF
SHIRLEY
BASSEY

RICHARD MR. PASTRY HEARNE · IVOR EMMANUEL
TOMMY FIELDS · THE CLARK BROS
* THE FABULOUS DANCING WATERS Etc *
STALLS 6·6 8·· 9·· CIRCLE 7·6 9·· BALCONY 3·6 5··

THE SHADOWS
.....In the Spotlight

Into the 1960's. The Blackpool Opera House was considered usually the best place for entertainment, certainly until the Hippodrome became the ABC Theatre in 1963. It was 1961 when Shirley Bassey shared top billing with Cliff and the Shadows at the theatre. Shirley covered July and August and Cliff and the gang took over on the 28th of the month until the end of the season. Shirley's biggest hit records were still to come. The soundtrack songs to the James Bond movies and the catchy 'Hey big spender' were a few years away yet. Cliff and the Shadows were, in 1961, the flavour of the month. As they took the stage that August, Cliff was at number 8 in the charts, the record was *'With a girl like you'*. Two earlier hits that year had been *'Gee whiz it's you'* and *'Theme for a dream'* in March and April respectively. The Shadows themselves were doing alright, *'Apache'* had sold incredibly well, staying at number one for six weeks. *'F.B.I'* reached the number four position in March of 1961 and *'Frightened City'* was at the number three position in June. As the Shadows began their stint at Blackpool on the 28th August 1961, *'Kon Tiki'* was sitting at no. 3 and selling fast. Even so, the record of the year turned out to be from that chap across the water....Elvis Presley. The film G.I. Blues was doing the rounds and the record *'Wooden Heart'* seemed to find its way into everybody's record collection in that glorious summer of 1961.

A PICTURE
of
JOE
BROWN

A letter of love
Comes the day
Stick around
People gotta talk

BEAUTIFUL DREAMER • ON LOVERS' HILL
I'LL CUT YOUR TAIL OFF • LOVERS' LANE   mono

DECCA
DFE 8500

Beautiful Dreamer
JOHN LEYTON

It was the year of change, the year pop stars took over the top of the bill spots at most of the theatres around the country and Blackpool as always was at the forefront of the latest events in entertainment in those years. We were on the eve of the Merseybeat sound taking Britain, and later the world, by storm. However, 1962 belonged really to the likes of Joe Brown, John Leyton, Billy Fury, Marty Wilde, Susan Maughan and Helen Shapiro. American stars also fared well, names like Bobby Vee and Johnny Tillotson are well remembered, from that year, as are the Drifters etc., What a time to be young !...............

The Screen Sizzles when
BILLY FURY
HELEN SHAPIRO
BOBBY VEE
PLAY IT COOL!

HEAR THESE HITS!
PLAY IT COOL
YOU'RE SWELL
ONCE UPON A DREAM
WHO CAN SAY
CRY MY HEART OUT
AT A TIME LIKE THIS
BUT I DON'T CARE
...and more!

Friday's only. The week of excursion train outings using the excellent value for money Town Holiday Runabout Rover tickets came to an end on the Friday. The leisurely start to the week with it's laid back easy morning starts and relaxed evening journey's home gave way on the Friday to a hectic day of dashing about trying to cram as much into the last day as possible. All day long there was a sense of urgency of being rushed, yet we did enjoy it and mum and dad had the following week to get over their travels before life at the mill beckoned them back to normality. On the Friday we would set off early and return quite late and it was always a very full day of activities. Friday of the holidays always began somewhat early. Dad and brother Bert would be out feeding the animals on dad's smallholding, known locally as 'The Ponderosa', not much after eight o'clock. With the back door of our house in Greenwood Terrace open, the summer sun would be flowing in and just across the way the hens would be noisily feeding and I would be busy sorting flasks out while mum was putting sandwiches together using numerous eggs supplied by those same hens just mentioned. Those egg and tomato butties still make my mouth water when I think of them. The smell from them, mixed with steam and the smell of burning coal wafting into a railway carriage is something I can always so easily recall. **(Above)** Abingdon Street looking towards Talbot Road.

BLACKPOOL NORTH

PLATFORMS 1 - 6
THIS WAY

PLATFORMS 7 - 16
IN QUEEN STREET

BRITISH RAILWAYS

BRITISH RAILWAYS

Reaching the North station. Well here we are, looking across from the corner of Dickson Road and Talbot Road. The main gates leading into the station and giving vehicle access draw your eyes to look into the train shed in the area near to numbers one and two platforms. The scene here doesn't look too busy but I always seem to recall there was a steady flow of traffic travelling by here even back in the 1950's and most certainly by the 1960's. Buses and coaches would be turning in and out of the bus station at Talbot Road. This tall concrete structure featured a multi story car park above the bus standing area and I think it dates from about the 1938 period. The concrete train shed over at the top of Queen Street which acted as the main buildings for the excursion platforms No's 7-16 was also built in 1938. There was much competition between the buses and the railways even in those pre-war years. My memory tells me we always seemed to enter the station in those 'dashing days' via the main gates rather than walking in through the archway on the station front, (see title page for better view of station frontage). Left we see the family , yes you've seen it before but for me to place them here along with the view of the station puts them in context with the views that I will hold forever in my mind of the way things were on those runabout daytrips to the Lancashire coast.

On the concourse. As we entered the station we briefly evaded the heat of the sun and left the noise of the streets of Blackpool behind. Once inside and making our way towards the concourse the noise of street life was exchanged for that of passengers, countless pairs of feet all seemingly moving at once. There was also the noise of staff trundling barrows about shouting and conversing with each other in the course of their duties. The occasional whistle on the platform would be acknowledged by a distant engine somewhere out of the train shed towards the platform end. Shafts of sunlight would stream down on the flagged concourse and a slight breeze could be felt as we passed the point where the main archway, lead out on to the station front and Dickson Road. As we neared the number five and six platforms we would pass close to the refreshment rooms and the sound of chinking cups could be heard and the smell of warm food would waft out onto the concourse making us hungry again. Other smells which always lingered were those of gas, burning coal, warm oil and in later years diesel fumes. Dad would quickly check the timings board, often pulling out a Players cigarette from his battered cigarette case and tapping it at both ends as he did. Quickly lighting it up he would usher us round towards the barrier on number five platform, his cigarette dangling from his mouth in a very Robert Mitcham sort of way. **(left)** Four of the station staff at Blackpool North who we would no doubt see in the 1950s and early 1960s, are seen here. The one at the far left (top) is Station Master Mr. T Dickinson, to his right is Inspector J W Hodgson. At the far left (bottom), is Ticket Inspector J E H Edwards and to his right is Leading Parcels Porter F L Turner. As the 1960's began, some 10,000 passengers would pass through Blackpool North station each Saturday between June and September.

On the Platforms

To the right we see the area by platform number two. There was a vehicle (carriage) roadway situated between number one and two platforms, the wall side number one platform quite often being filled with parcel vans and the like, in the process of being loaded or unloaded. **(below)** This view taken from number five platform shows the building detail as we look back towards the barriers. The refreshment rooms are over to the right and the train crew mess room is nearer the camera. As we reached the barrier, dad would be organised as usual, he would have pulled out the runabout tickets and arranged them in a fan ready to show the ticket man on the barrier. Sending us all in front of him he would motion to the chap checking tickets and say *'they're all theer Jock'* and with that we would be waved onto the platform from where it was a short walk up to number six platform, the left hand wallside one.

Beneath the roof

There, I told you the sun came streaming down. It bathed the platforms in light just the way it did on the concourse. However, platforms number two and three are not that well illuminated and the reason for this is that these were the two main arrival platforms and as such when the engines backed out their own coaches as was often the case in later years, the fires on the engines needed a little tending to after the run in from Poulton and the draw on the fires as the engines got stuck into the reversing move sent the smoke up into the roof blackening the glass roof panels and also the end windows. Picture by *Michelle Howe*

BLACKPOOL NORTH

Off to Fleetwood. Off we go then to Fleetwood market. As we see above, the weather wasn't always sunny and bright. There were days of drizzle when we would have to get out the 'pacamacs'. Some years were noteably bad for rain when we seemed to spend hours trailing round stores bored to tears in a effort to stay warm and dry. Thankfully the fair weather years were far greater in number overall. The two really wet years I recall are 1962 and 1964. The Sputnicks and space probes got blamed for those, the 1962 summer weather failure attributed to the launching of the satellite Telstar. **42431** is the engine seen above awaiting departure, very much like the way our 'tanky' would be simmering away before our departure to Fleetwood. Talbot Road's large goods warehouse is visible in the distance as is the No. 3 signal box. **(right)** The view from the compartment shows the old train heating boiler that was always to be seen on its own siding between the two parts of the station.

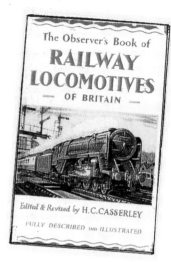

Leaving the North station. Blackpool driver Jim Hardy, a well known character in steam days, is seen here on the platform at the North station in front of engine **45538** *Giggleswick*. He was a leading light in the running of the Loco Club that was located behind Central Drive and following his retirement in the 1960/61 period, he could be found there most days officiating in club affairs. He always liked a tidy footplate and was one of those enginemen whose 'drills' were as clean at the end of the week as they were at the start. Over on **page 81** we see engineman Jacky White setting off. **Above** is **45705** *Seahorse* waiting to leave platform 3. Pictures by *Don Rutter* and *Peter Fitton*.

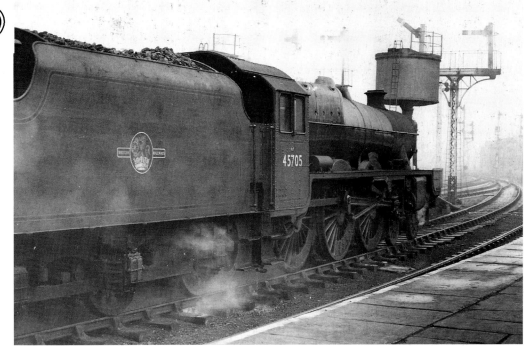

BLACKPOOL NORTH

As we depart from the North station we may as well briefly look at some of the staff and machinery that made up the every day scene in the days of our outings from Blackpool North. Banks Street Goods was the term given to the sidings and loading dock area over on the far left side of the station, beyond the excursion platforms. Parcels were handled here, advance luggage at one time came in here by the van full and the sidings were usually well filled with vans of one sort or another.

(above) A group of staff take time off to pose for a picture; they are Len Booth, Frank Bennett and Jack Cookson who were all van drivers. Bob Grisedale (in the middle) was a parcels inspector and Tommy Kirkham on the right was a parcels porter.

(below) On the 19th July 1959, Peter Fitton visited the North station and shed, etc., In the siding up to the houses in Lang Street and Wall Street was a train load of horse boxes being shunted by one of the little Stanier class 3 tank engines. Peter's trusty push bike is resting against the wall in the bottom left of the picture. Possibly the next part of Peter's bike ride would take him round Back Ashburton Road to the main entrance and lobby of Blackpool North engine shed.

Pictures by *Jack Cookson* and *Peter Fitton*

Local Trip and Shunt engines

(right) The little Stanier Class 3 tank engines were a favourite of mine at Blackpool as well as at Southport. By the 1950's they had been replaced on passenger duties all over the country by the far superior steaming Ivatt Class 2 tanks. The modern tank engines with their self cleaning smoke boxes and hopper ash pans etc., were welcomed with open arms by shed staff. So the little Staniers essentially became trip and shunt engines. Both Blackpool's and Southport's allocations had been there quite some years with the odd exception. In the course of this volume you will find pictures and details of these bonny little engines on pages 95 and 122/123. Here we see **40109** on the North shed coal stage road in March 1961. Only two of Blackpool's were steamed in the spring of 1961 and 40109 was one of them.

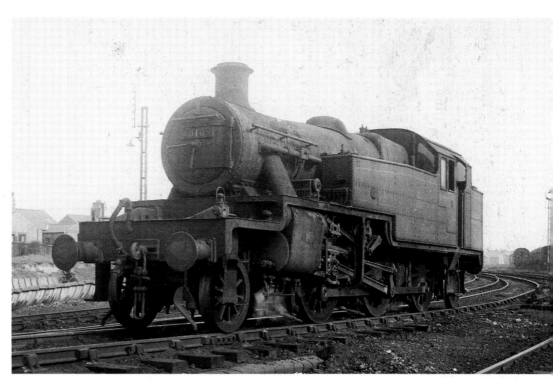

(below) Lanky 'A' class engines back in LMS days still performed many passenger turns and locally did much in the way of excursion train work, but by the 1950's their days as a whole were numbered. Not because they were life expired. No, you simply couldn't wear these old girls out. They were truly built to stand anything. They were basic, they were open to the elements and crews as you can appreciate liked a bit of shelter and comfort, but they did steam well as a rule. Getting the injectors on at times could prove a problem but nothing that a bucket of cold water and some bundles of cotton waste wouldn't solve. Blackpool North managed to keep hold of three of these sturdy little engines until the 1958/59 period. They were 52415, 52466 and 52523. The one we see here **52466**, was filmed on the North shed on the 25th July 1958, but by February 1959 she had gone to Oldham Lees depot. Also on the shed on the same day was 52523, which moved to Bolton in November 1958 and stayed active until 1962. The last of the three, 52415, which was a regular on the coast line shunts, also went to Bolton in January 1959, but had been sent to Horwich for scrap by the summer of 1960. Pictures by *Peter Fitton* and *Frank Dean*

Talbot Road Goods. At the start of the 1960's, small diesel shunt engines began to appear. The larger 350hp shunters were already with us, the numerous classes of little diesel shunters that came around the 1960/61 time were designed to be of use in the docks and goods depots where tight curves prevailed. Above we see the type allocated for use at Fleetwood and at Talbot Road goods yard and coal yard. The Yorkshire Engine Company made them and they were a simple 170hp machine, solid but not up to much. Driver Albert Durrant was on them regularly, as we see in both the pictures above. Shunters Ron Singleton and Malcom Handforth are also in the left hand view. **(below)** Albert is doing a spot of pretend fishing, he must think he is on the end of the North Pier. Assisting him are Malcolm Handforth and Driver Alan Jackson. Alan is seen 'having a fiver' as enginemen would say outside the mess cabin at Talbot Road. With a nice cup of China tea. How do we know it is China tea ?.... because of the 'junk' floating on the top !......... all pictures by *Don Rutter*.

BEWARE
OF
SHUNTING

A VISIT TO BLACKPOOL NORTH SHED

We'll be on our way soon to Fleetwood, but not before we pay a visit to the North shed, to see the way things were in the years of the 1950's and up to 1962. Above we see the excursion platforms No's. 7-16 with the lines leading into the main part of North station over to the left. Blackpool North No. 3 signal box is visible and behind it stands the ornate structure of the Ramsden Arms Hotel, the favoured watering hole of most enginemen locally. A Royal Scot engine looks to be standing on a train in platform No. 7;
(below) On 20th September 1952, the Northern Rubber Company's annual outing brought to Blackpool North, Eastern Region A1 Pacific **60113** *Great Northern*. The engine is seen posing by the shed on what was called 'the back road', which was the loop around the carriage sidings at Enfield Road.

Picture of 60113 by *Frank Dean*

On shed, Easter Saturday 1959. Although Blackpool North never catered for the volume of engines you would see just across town at Blackpool Central depot, the North shed nevertheless could quite often boast a decent variety of motive power during the summer season throughout the 1950's and into the early 1960's. Obviously in the later 1960's when Blackpool Central had closed, the North shed came into its own and by the last real year of steam, 1966, there were times when you would find the biggest surviving selection of former LMS express power to be found anywhere, all queuing in line for a turn on the table at Enfield Road. On 28th of March 1959, it seems as if a bit of a Scottish invasion was taking place. **45720** *Indomitable* sits by the side of sister engine **45707** *Valiant.* Both these engines were based at Corkerhill shed in Glasgow and from where they had brought excursions. In the next few years these Scottish 5X's became a rarity, only coming out of store for a series of summer outings each year, usually to Blackpool. They were all condemned in the last months of 1962 in line with policy decisions relating to the retention of summer only engines and coaching stock. Standard Five **73099** seen to the left was also a Glasgow engine from Polmadie depot and behind her was **72005** *Clan McGregor* of Carlisle Kingmoor shed which had also arrived with Glasgow traffic. **(left)** Blackpool's Billy Blundell gazes out of the cab window with those dazzling blue eyes of his, no doubt contemplating the shift ahead. Look out for him oiling round 45694 *Bellerophon* in the reprise volume in the last years of steam.

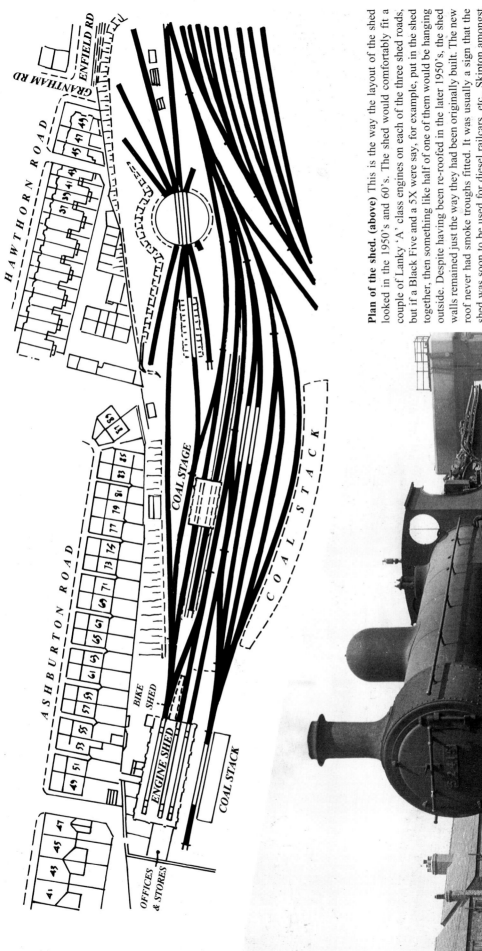

Plan of the shed. (above) This is the way the layout of the shed looked in the 1950's and 60's. The shed would comfortably fit a couple of Lanky 'A' class engines on each of the three shed roads, but if a Black Five and a 5X were say, for example, put in the shed together, then something like half of one of them would be hanging outside. Despite having been re-roofed in the later 1950's, the shed walls remained just the way they had been originally built. The new roof never had smoke troughs fitted. It was usually a sign that the shed was soon to be used for diesel railcars, etc., Skipton amongst other depots was also never supplied fully with troughing, it even had recesses in the pits where electric light tubes were to be fitted in diesel days but this never happened. Blackpool North shed would in time play host to railcars as a stabling point but only for a few years. Following the closure of the Central station and Rigby Road motive power depot, the North shed briefly for the 1965 season became swamped with excursion engines but by the following year 1966, a great many summer extra trains had been knocked off and as a result servicing the arriving engines became easily manageable. By 1967 the specials had dwindled out of all recognition and big diesel engines far outnumbered the steam engines sitting on the shed. All of these later years will be looked at in detail in the reprise edition. **(below) 52415** looks fit for another 20 years or so as she sits on No. 1 shed road. Steam finished about ten years after this view was taken so it is easy to say that given a bit of care, these old ladies of steam could have survived to the end, if there had been enough work to go round.

Picture by *Frank Dean*

ENFIELD RD

GRANTHAM RD

HAWTHORN ROAD

ASHBURTON ROAD

COAL STAGE

COAL STACK

COAL STACK

BIKE SHED

ENGINE SHED

OFFICES & STORES

Class 2 (Ivatt) 2-6-2T No. 41249 [W. Vaughan-Jenkins

Class 6P5F (Stanier) 2-6-0 No. 42970 [Brian E. Morrison

Class 2 (Riddles) 2-6-2T No. 84012 [Brian E. Morrison

Class 6P5F (Hughes-Fowler) 2-6-0 No. 42854 [D. Penney

Class 3 (Riddles) 2-6-2T No. 82016 [P. Ransr

6P5F (Hughes-Fowler) 2-6-0 No. 42829 (with Reidinger rotary poppet valve gear) [K. R. Pirt

A BRACE OF POPPET - VALVE CRABS
AT BLACKPOOL NORTH

Easter outing 1960 (18/4/60). To see one of Burton's rare poppet valve 'Crab' 2-6-0's at Blackpool was a real novelty, but to see two on the same day was in the words of Eddie Cochran *'Something else'*. On Easter Monday 1960, both **42822** and **42824** were captured on film on the North shed by Peter Fitton. Peter had snapped 42824 passing Kirkham on the fast line, as we saw on page 21. There were five poppet valve fitted engines in total, No's. 42818/822/824/825 and 42829. They had been shedded at Burton on Trent for years and by the end of the 1950's, they were beginning to spend a lot of time in store. All would be withdrawn in 1962 between May and July, having been stored unserviceable since the end of the 1961 summer timetable. 42818 and 42822 went to Horwich Works for scrap in May and June of 1962. 42824/825/829 followed in September. You may recall 42825 was on the cover of part one in this series. Don't worry about what's behind the ABC book on page 88, this excellent view of the North shed by Peter Fitton is also the cover picture for the reprise volume, the final book in this series. All pictures here by *Peter Fitton*

Class 6P5F (Hughes-Fowler) 2-6-0 No. 42785

[P. H. Groom

Class 2 (Ivatt) 2-6-0 No. 46501

[J. Cupit

Class 6P5F (Hughes-Fowler) 2-6-0 No. 42822 (with Reidinger rotary poppet valve gear)

[J. Cupit

Class 4 (Ivatt) 2-6-0 No. 43154

[B. K. B. Green

Class 6P5F (Stanier) 2-6-0 No. 42979

[B. K. B. Green

Class 4 (Riddles) 2-6-0 No. 76088

[K. R. Pirt

RCTS VISIT 24.9.60

'Spotters' club visit. The Railway Travel and Correspondence Society paid a visit to the North shed on Saturday 24th of September 1960. It was the 'Lights' season and as always there was a good selection of engines to be seen. Frank Dean's diary, made up of notes of the pictures he took, is to the left here. The engines filmed at the Central shed are on the left page and those on the North shed such as 73091, etc., are on the right hand page. As you can see, Frank took pictures of the engines seen on the next few pages, Peter Fitton and the gang were their too and they are Peter's pictures which illustrate for us the scenes on the shed that day. The only exception to this is the view above taken by Arnold Battson of **45653** *Barham*.

Resting in the sun. Having been turned, their fires cleaned and drawn up under the firehole door, and having had the ashpan emptied, engines would be watered and the coal would be pulled down ready for the return trip. Shed men would have a departure plan to work to and would line engines up according to their time off shed. Both the engines here are resting ready for the journey home, **above** we see **45720** *Indomitable* again and **below** is **72003** *Clan Fraser*, which seems to be still in reverse gear as it stands on the coal storage road. The lines here by the coal yard would in later years be filled with Type 4 diesel engines, with hardly a steamer in sight. It was amazing how quickly the shed scene changed in just a handful of years. Pictures by *Peter Fitton*

Overlooking Enfield Road. The Gresley K3 2-6-0's were a familiar sight at Blackpool right up until the 1962 season ended, as we have pointed out in earlier volumes. Mostly they would be found over at the Central shed at Rigby Road or Bloomfield sidings, but now and again they would turn up at the North shed. **61904** was always at Hull and the 1960 season was to be her last. The locomotive is standing on one of the roads off the turntable overlooking Enfield Road. Only a couple of old sleepers and a pile of ash are in use as a stop block and it is a steep drop down the banking into Enfield Road.
Picture by *Peter Fitton*

HALF-DAY EXCURSIONS
TO **BLACKPOOL**

Turning *Barham* **24th September 1960.** Just a few feet away from where 61904 was resting and swinging round on the 65 foot turntable was Blackpool's own 5X, **45653** *Barham*. She looked really well, nicely 'bulled' up and still sporting the old lion and wheel emblem, but the pile of nutty slack in the tender won't go far on a 5X, especially with an heavy handed driver. Contrary to safe engine working, she seems to be still in back gear whilst going round on the table !!!... The engine had worked the 1/40pm Manchester Victoria to Blackpool North SO service that day and had arrived on shed at about 3/40pm. Waiting in the queue for the turntable were 42861, 44658 and 73091. Picture by *Peter Fitton*

Stranger from Salop 24/9/60. As the queue for the turntable shortened and 42861 took its turn, 44658 was moved up ready and the last in the line was this superb lined green Standard Class Five from Shrewsbury No.**73091**. Seeing ordinary Standard engines in green was a real treat, they were always special. If you look back towards the last years of steam certain 'green-uns' became celebrities, 73029 and 73092 on the Southern, 73014 and 73026 at Bolton and going back slightly further those Somerset and Dorset one's turned out from Eastleigh works quickly spring to mind.. They were 73049/51/52/54 and the Western one 73068 and of the class 4 variety, I well recall us getting 75020/21/26 and 75027 in green livery ex-Cambrian lines on the Grassington branch trains in 1967/68. Shrewsbury shed had a number of Standard

Class Fives including 73090-98. They all eventually moved away, 73091 going to Gloucester for the rest of its brief working life up to July of 1965. On the 24th September 1960, 73091 set off back from Blackpool North with empty stock and we showed her passing Kirkham and Wesham on the Up fast line on page 105 of part four in this series.

Picture by *Peter Fitton*

Scottish weekend, Sunday 24th September 1961. One year on from 1960 and the RCTS paid another visit to the North shed. The 'Lights' were on and it was Scottish weekend. There were seven specials from Glasgow and one from Balloch which all came into the North and a number of others which terminated over at the Central station. Also arriving at the North station on Saturday 23rd of September were four specials from Birmingham and one from Walsall, as well as others from local starting points around Lancashire. The Scottish visitors had set off on Friday night and were booked via Preston EL and Todd Lane Junction to be re-manned by local crews before setting out from Preston for Blackpool. They began arriving at 5.55am on Saturday morning with 1X75 from Glasgow Central (45112).

1X73 came next at 6.4am (72005) also from Glasgow Central. At 6.10am, 73079 appeared with 1X78 from Glasgow St.Enoch. Also from the same station came 1X74 which arrived at 6.20am (ten minutes late) with 45673 *Keppel* on the front end. 45727 *Inflexible*, all coaled up and ready for that return trip to Scotland. There are some lovely cobs of coal in the tender, which will no doubt fizzle and bang as the fire is made up on Monday. Around the 1961 period, Glasgow's Corkerhill shed had Jubilee Class No's. 45621/665/673/677/687/692/693/707 /711/720 and 45721. All were wiped off the books in the cull of steam engines in the last months of 1962. Some of those which turned up at Blackpool in September of 1961 were more than likely making their last outings before storage and withdrawal. Picture here by *Paul Claxton*

5pm. Three relief trains also ran to Glasgow, two were booked jobs and one was a 'Q' timed special. All ran to Glasgow Central or St Enoch stations. Above, we see No. 45727 *Inflexible*, all coaled up and ready for that return trip to Scotland. There are some lovely cobs of coal in the tender, which will no doubt fizzle and bang as the fire is made up on Monday. Around the 1961 period, Glasgow's Corkerhill shed had Jubilee Class No's. 45621/665/673/677/687/692/693/707 /711/720 and 45721. All were wiped off the books in the cull of steam engines in the last months of 1962. Some of those which turned up at Blackpool in September of 1961 were more than likely making their last outings before storage and withdrawal. Picture here by *Paul Claxton*

Inflexible with 1X80 followed *Keppel* into the North station. 1X77 came next at 6.45am, sadly we don't have an engine listed for that one. 45680 *Camperdown* turned up at 6.50am with the special 1X82 from Balloch. At 7.5am, 45170 brought in 1X79 from Glasgow Central. The Birmingham excursions and the one from Walsall all arrived at varying times up to 11.50am that Saturday morning. The Scottish 'Lights' specials didn't run back while the Monday afternoon. (25th September). They began leaving at five minutes past two in steady intervals up to

Talking of Tanks

As mentioned in earlier volumes, the little Stanier Class 3 tanks were a familiar sight at Blackpool and Southport until 1961/62. As station pilots and carriage shunters, Blackpool used the type until the end of the 1960 season when just about all of them were stored. Only two worked locally in 1961, 40109 and 40174. Over at Southport it was a similar affair. You would see them but not in use. What had happened is that diesel railcars had now taken over passenger services and the Stanier and Fairburn 2-6-4 tank engines were surplus to requirements, so the little Stanier tanks were simply laid up. The class four tanks replaced them for the 1961 summer and 42558, 42625 and 42148 became regular pilots amongst others at Blackpool in the next few years.

End of the line for the little Staniers. In March of 1961, there were eight of the little 'tankies' still on the Fylde. 40109 was in steam on the North shed, while 40072/99/174 were stored there serviceable. Over at the Central shed on the long road by the sand dryer were 40091 with damaged framing at one side and 40166. Round at Fleetwood was 40164 which was in a steamable condition and saw limited use in April and May of 1961 on the odd local passenger job. 40103 was also there stored, never to work again. 40091 and 40166 were cleared out of the Central shed and taken up to Fleetwood. About the same time, 40099 left the North shed for Lower Darwen, (May 1961). 40174 went to Preston (Lostock Hall), then later into Preston shed for storage. 40072 and 40109 moved into the shed at Fleetwood along with 40164 and stayed there dormant until the back end of 1961. Both 40072 and 40164 left to join 40099 at Blackburn. This left the last steamable engine in the shed as 40109. Into 1962 and 40109 was still in Fleetwood shed, although out of use with 40091/166/103 stored outside along with 43502. They set off for the scrap yard at Wigan on 19th July 1962, after which 40109 took their place outside of the shed (see pages 122/123). It would be April 1963 before this last little Stanier tank headed off for Scotland and the breakers yard of George Campbell's at Airdrie. Sister engines from Lower Darwen, 40072/99 had already been dealt with in Campbell's yard when 40109 arrived. Seen here are 40072 and 40099 on the North shed on the 3rd March 1961. Pictures by *Peter Fitton*

The Saturday after Scottish weekend in 1961 was a real day to remember. On Saturday the 30th September, as the nights drew in quickly and the air grew ever colder, the Northern Rubber Company's annual outing to the seaside brought to Blackpool North the world's fastest steam engine, **60022** *Mallard*. The rubber company's special 1X08 from Retford was preceded by another 'Lights' excursion which used unusual motive power, this turning out to be the restored Midland Railway Compound loco. No.1000, which was used as a pilot engine on 1T07 from Stoke Golding. This train had 45548 *Lytham St. Annes* as the train engine and the formation of the train included two sleeping

cars. The special from Retford with *Mallard* came via the Calder Valley, Copy Pit and down through East Lancashire. Rose Grove driver Rennie Lonsdale was to act as a conductor from Sowerby Bridge and was offered the driving seat so he drove all the way to Blackpool North and took the engine on to the shed. It was a proud Rennie who played on the chime whistle passing his home depot at Rose Grove that September Saturday in 1961. Above we see *Mallard* at rest on the shed at Blackpool after travelling as far as Poulton to turn on the 'triangle' there. 45387, is seen to the left. Also on shed were 45033, 42643, 45436, 44936, 42928, 45702 *Colossus*, 42638, 45146, 42294, 45395,

45685 *Barfleur*, 45584 *North West Frontier*, 45410, 45431, 42559, 45540 *Sir Robert Turnbull*, 45600 *Bermuda*, 46137 *Prince of Wales Volunteers (South Lancashire)*, 45548 *Lytham St.Annes* and the Midland Compound No.1000. The days excitement ended in fine style just before midnight when the Compound piloted *Mallard* away from Blackpool North with the Northern Rubber special for Retford. In the cold crisp night air they must have sounded as well as they looked as they eased away leaving the illuminated Tower and the glittering lights of Blackpool behind them.

*Picture of Mallard by **Paul Claxton***

L.M.S. LOCOMOTIVES OF THE PAST

Standard Class 5 4-6-0 No. 73166 [P. H. Groom]

Dealey Midland Class 4P 4-4-0 compound No. 1000 (preserved in working order). [R. J. Buckley]

Standard Class 4 4-6-0 No. 75031 [J. E. Wilkinson]

Johnson Midland Class 3P 4-4-0 No. 719 [L.P.C.]

Standard Class 9F 2-10-0 No. 92084 [P. H. Groom]

Johnson Midland 4-2-2 No. 124 [L.P.C.]

COMBINED VOLUME
BRITISH RAILWAYS
LOCOMOTIVES
an Ian Allan a b c
COMBINED VOLUME 10/6

Frank Dean's film diary again provides us with an insight into the events of certain dates. In this instance, it is the 29th and 30th September 1961. 45727 *Indomitable* was back at the resort again from Glasgow and was seen on the 28th September working the 9.15am to Manchester and on the 29th (Friday), it was working the 9.55am from Blackpool to Crewe. Not bad considering it only went back home to Scotland on Monday the 25th September. As the notes show, the old Midland Railway Compound 4-4-0 No.1000 (seen above in the ABC), brought in excursion 1T07 from Stoke Golding with 45548 *Lytham St.Annes*. The combined volume of locomotives seen at the top was the one which had just come out at the time of the *Mallard* and Compound visit to Blackpool. Diesels had begun to dominate the covers of these well known spotters' books, thankfully the 1963 one had A4 No. 60017 on the cover in a striking painting by Vic Welch.

45548

'Lytham St. Annes'

What an ideal choice of engine to use on the 'Lights' special, choosing 45548 was indeed very fitting. It is now believed this was most likely the engines last outing anywhere, as in October 1961, 45548 was placed in store with the other Patriot class engines at Rugby. Finally withdrawn in June 1962, she was broken up at Crewe works just about a year after her epic last run to the 'Lights' at Blackpool.

Looking good

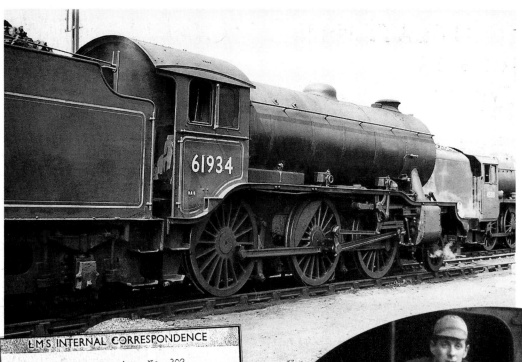

Ardsley K3 No. **61934**, sits in the sun on Blackpool North shed on Saturday 9th June 1962. Maybe the engine was on loan to Low Moor at Bradford as a replacement for my old favourite 61975, which capsized at the end of the 1961 season following numerous hammerings over Copy Pit and other similar arduous routes. The paintwork is good, as are the tyres and the bottom end of the loco. There looks to be a lot of mileage left in this Gresley legacy. Come November 1962, just a few short months away, 61934 shuffled off to Doncaster for dismantling, what a tragedy and what a sad time it was in the run up to the Beeching years.

Picture by *Peter Fitton*

LMS INTERNAL CORRESPONDENCE

To   Fireman D. Dunstan, No. 302,
     Blackpool M.P.D.

From: Motive Power Depot, Blackpool.
         15.8.62.   (Centre No.   )

FIREMEN FOR PASSING TO ACT AS DRIVERS.

A certificate to act as a driver has been issued and you may be utilised accordingly forthwith as and when necessary.

FOR J. A. Owen

Please call in office – to sign book regarding Permanent Notices.

In the driving seat. (above) A confirmation slip advises Dougie Dunstan that having successfully passed his exam to act as a driver, he must now be ready to take over the driving seat as and when requested. Passed men usually had the best route cards, they would quickly sign the routes everywhere practicable in order to get all the spare driving turns possible. **(right)** Doug looks happy and confident as he leans out of the cab of Rebuilt 'Scot', *The Rifle Brigade* at Euston station. When Blackpool Central closed in 1964, Dougie made a move to Crewe to further his career as there seemed little future of promotion locally. We have reached the end of our look at the North shed and on Sunday 16th December 1962, **45697** *Achilles*, was stored in good order by the ash pit. It was a bitter cold Christmas that year and New Year 1963 proved to be dramatic in many ways and I am not just talking about the weather. Picture by *Peter Fitton*

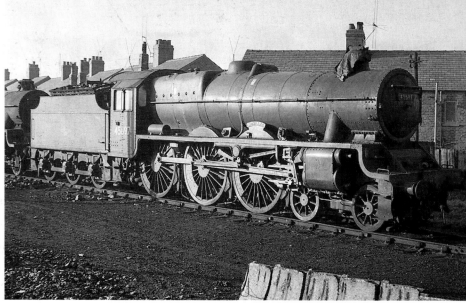

FLEETWOOD FOOTPLATEMAN
- TONY BRETHERTON

Turning Ken Bradshaw's Fleetwood line memories into a visual thing would have been no easy task if we hadn't have had the excellent pictures supplied by Fleetwood engineman Tony Bretherton. Tony's 'working 'scenes, together with Chris Spring's superb documentary views of the stations along the line etc., combine to show us the whole picture. If Tony hadn't decided simply to take a few pictures of his workmates, realising as he did that it was all shortly coming to an end, then the next sixty or so pages would be decidedly lacking in that most important of ingredients, the human element. Tony Bretherton is seen on the left on 45444 and his old driver below is Tony Bradshaw, Ken's namesake, who we'll be seeing more of as we journey to Fleetwood. Pictures here by *Tony Bretherton*

On the move

Here we go then with the final portion of this book, the run to Fleetwood. As you headed out of Blackpool, it seemed to take ages to leave the 'feel of Blackpool' behind. Even at Layton there were many red brick houses, the buses you'd see were still the cream and green painted ones that plied the street of the resort and the over bridge at Layton station, which carried Plymouth Road across the railway at right angles, had a retaining wall and abutments along it's span that reminded you of the one at Squires Gate station on the coast line.

Leaving Layton behind, and making for Carleton Crossing, it would be a slight pull for our little tank engine as we could hear it barking away and then whistling on the approach to the crossing. Over on the left side as we had set out from Layton, you would have been able to see the old brick works and quarry by the lineside. By the later 1960's the old quarry part was filled in with hundreds of tons of rubble and waste from the demolished R.H.O Hills store in Blackpool which was gutted by fire in 1967. Just short of Carleton Crossing at the highest point of the line, if you looked back across to the coast, then you'd be able to see the tower that was on the top of the 'Miners Home' and clearly make out the mock-castle effect on the buildings of the Norbreck Castle Hotel on the north promenade. After climbing to Carleton Crossing our little engine would be eased back and could be seen ahead of us swaying gently, side to side, as we dropped down by the fields towards Poulton No. 4 signal box. Clouds of steam from the chimney top carried by the wind would drift across the fields where the cows were grazing in the bright sunshine and the smell would waft it's way back into the compartment. Bearing steadily to the left we would take the curve round towards the site of Poulton Curve Halt. The neat little station, seen in better times across on page 101, had closed in December 1952 and all I ever remember is the overgrown remnants of the platforms. **(above)** At the top we see the station buildings at Layton on the Up side. **(left)** A view from the train about to pass beneath Plymouth road at Layton and Tony Bradshaw gets ready to brake for Poulton Curve. Bottom view by *Tony Bretherton*

Poulton Curve Halt. (above) Once past Poulton No. 4 signal box, we would leave the main line to Preston and curve away towards Thornton. The angle round to Poulton No. 5 had a speed limit of 35mph and there was quite often much squealing and grinding as we took the curve on dry summer days. **45574** *India* is seen passing Poulton No. 4 on it's way into Blackpool North with the 9.4am SO working from Crewe, so the time it was seen here at Poulton would be around 11.30am. The line to Fleetwood is the one seen in between the signal box and the Blackpool bound train W389. **(below)** Ivatt Class 2 No. **41280** runs into Poulton Curve Halt on a working from Fleetwood to Blackpool North in June 1952. The shelters were based on a design dating back to L&Y days. Note also the 'Hawkeseye' station 'running-in' board, an LMS provision.

Picture by H Townley

'Tanky'
at Poulton Curve

Working the Westinghouse. Ken Bradshaw spent many happy hours on the push-pull tank jobs between Blackpool, Fleetwood, Poulton and Kirkham. **10802**, seen right at Poulton Curve Halt, in September 1946, was one that Ken remembers well. He taught many a young lad to fire and practice their driving abilities on these 'tanky' turns. Whilst running along on his own on the engine Ken, with pipe in mouth, would be busy cleaning down the 'Dolly' (grained cab roof) or polishing the brasswork with a piece of mole skin on a stick. When leaving stations with the Westinghouse pump working, drivers would just be unaware up front if the engine was getting too much steam and about to slip. Ken would then use the brass slide handle to retard the opening of the regulator to prevent wheel spin.

The Ivatts take over. The revolutionary range of modern locomotives by H.A.Ivatt that appeared during the last years of the LMS formed the basis of a number of the later BR Standard designs. The overall appeal of the engines was easy day to day maintenance and a better working atmosphere for the crew. The Class 2 tender and tank engines were universally liked wherever they went. The Class 4 2-6-0's weren't just as clever, the brake blocks squealed, they steamed erratically and pitched and rolled at speed, but at least the cabs were cosy. The Ivatt Class 2 tender engines first appeared at Blackpool in 1948, followed soon after in 1950/51 by the tank engine variety. They quickly took over the duties of the old 'Lanky' Radial tanks on the local passenger turns. By the early 1950's all the fourteen 'Lanky' tanks allocated to Fleetwood had gone into store, many never working again. Those based at Blackpool also fell out of use. Across on page 102, engine No. **6412**, one of the new Class 2 tender engines, calls at Poulton Curve on the 30th April 1948.

Bunker first. The modern BR Standard tanks, which came in the 1950's, and the Ivatt Class 2 tank engines which arrived slightly earlier, were all well liked on these little shuttle turns. Easy to fire, good water pumps, rocking fire grates, etc., they even rode well running bunker first, just like bigger 2-6-4 tank engines. On 11th May 1963, **84016,** en-route from Poulton to Fleetwood, passes over the junction where the lines converge from the Blackpool direction. The little two coach train is a portion of a combined Manchester to Blackpool North and Fleetwood service. **(below)** A similar train is about to pass the same point though some years earlier on 23rd June 1951 with **41282** on the front. Pictures by *Peter Fitton* and *Frank Dean*

(above) Towards the end of the steam era on the local passenger services, **42445** takes the line round to Poulton station. The train is just passing beneath Gerrards Terrace road bridge and the line in the foreground leads to Blackpool. It is the 23rd July 1964 and the tank engine will reverse at Poulton ready for the last part of the journey into Blackpool North. **(below)** Just on the Thornton side of Gerrards Terrace road bridge, the 2/50 Broad Street fish train with **45442** on the front end gets a clear run into Poulton. If you check the map on page 105, you will notice how the line from Poulton No. 5 signal box sweeps first to the right then to the left to join the original formation of the railway for the run towards Tarngate. The line then ran almost in a straight line all the way to Thornton and Burn Naze. Now, briefly, we really were out in the countryside. Passing smallholdings and farm land on both sides, we would approach and pass Tarngate crossing. Not a block signalling post, it was simply a 'gate box', that was just about three quarters of a mile from Poulton No. 5 signal box. We were now travelling on a slight embankment, if we leant out and looked along past the engine, in the distance about a third of a mile away, the tall signals protecting Thornton level crossing and the gates of that crossing were easy to see. With the signals against us at times, road traffic would be steadily crossing the railway on Victoria Road East at Thornton. As we neared Thornton, we were suddenly back in a built up area of housing and shops, and close by the crossing on the right was a school throng with children running and shouting in the dinner time break from lessons. Pictures here by *Peter Fitton*

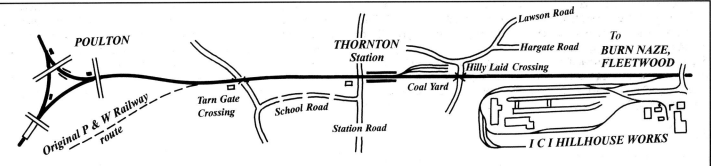

Entering
Thornton station

On the Up side platform at Thornton and looking back towards Poulton, you can see the signals protecting Tarngate crossing, just down the line. The school mentioned on page 104 is hidden to the left behind the signal box and the station masters house. The shops on the right which included the 'Candy Box' sweet shop always seemed busy, note the stone in the wall above them; it read WOODLAND PLACE 1900. Further along was a chip shop, the smell of which was ever present to us on our outings as we usually entered Thornton during dinner time. The engine here is **84018** and the train on this occasion is the 11.59am from Poulton to Fleetwood on Saturday 10th August 1964.   Picture by **Chris Spring**

THORNTON - CLEVELEYS

PASSENGERS MUST
CROSS THE LINE
BY THE BRIDGE

Thornton station

(above) The station signal box still looks in good order in this 1960's view. As soon has our little train had slipped into the platform, the signalman would quickly wind the barrel wheel to open the gates and with a clatter they would lock against their guides and road traffic would start rolling again. The Station Master's house is just visible on the right.

(left) A happy looking Tony Bradshaw rests his hand on the regulator of his little tank engine, happy days !.....

Thornton platforms. (above) The Up side platform is seen to better effect in this picture. Thornton was quite a modern station and looked very similar in design to St. Annes on the coast line. Built in 1928, the buildings were quite substantial and the platforms lengthy. They could handle trains up to twelve coaches in length and were straight throughout their length, giving better operating safety. **(below)** This 1962 view from the crossing is taken looking along towards Hilly Laid gate crossing box. Thornton's Down starting signal and the distant signal for Hilly Laid are easy to spot. Further in the distance towards Burn Naze is the home board at Hilly Laid and the distant signal for Burn Naze. Between the station at Thornton and Hilly Laid Crossing was a coal yard on the left, known as Brown's. When Ken Bradshaw left Thornton on the last leg into Fleetwood, he would give his mum a whistle, one long and one short after passing over Hilly Laid Crossing. She knew then to get his meal ready, allowing him time to put the engine away and travel home on his motor bike. She often waved to him from the back door of No. 12 Hargate Road.

By the Booking Hall. This is the way the area by the barrier looked in the 1960's. The chalk board listing train times mounted up by the left hand ticket office window still bears the symbol LMS at the top, whilst the later BR board below it advises about season tickets and increased charges of which there were many as Beeching's band of followers tried to balance the books. By the time this view was taken staff levels would be at an all time low, cleaning and maintenance was rapidly going downhill. On page 109 we see the station frontage. Station Master big Archie Buchanan, the Booking Office and a glimpse of the seaside, Cleveleys style.

Big Archie. In the Buchanan family circle, dad was Big Archie (seen above) and son Archie was Little Archie. Mr. Buchanan senior is pictured on the garden path of the family home in Rossendale Avenue North in Thornton. He was station master at Thornton in the years 1940-47. Then station master at Poulton from 1947 to about 1960. A move then followed to Blackburn as chief goods agent. He retired to New Zealand in 1966

THORNTON - CLEVELEYS

CLEVELEYS

THORNTON - CLEVELEYS

WAY
OUT

THORNTON - CLEVELEYS

Thornton........
a final glimpse

Across on page 110, we see the entrance to the station on the Down side via the main buildings. The lower picture shows the barriers on the Down side, leading along to the footbridge staircase. **(above)** A last look in the Booking Hall area, this time looking in the opposite direction to the view on page 108. Finally, on the right is the Down side platform by the stairway leading to the footbridge.

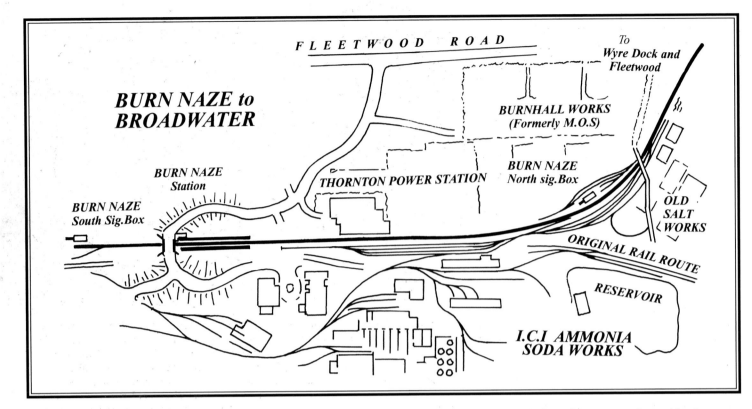

FLEETWOOD ROAD

To
Wyre Dock and
Fleetwood

**BURN NAZE to
BROADWATER**

BURNHALL WORKS
(Formerly M.O.S)

BURN NAZE
Station

BURN NAZE
North sig. Box

THORNTON POWER STATION

OLD
SALT
WORKS

BURN NAZE
South Sig. Box

ORIGINAL RAIL ROUTE

RESERVOIR

I.C.I AMMONIA
SODA WORKS

Passing Hillhouse Works

As we read at the beginning of this book Ken Bradshaw's family moved to No.12 Hargate Road Thornton, when dad, Bert Bradshaw took a position as head of the boiler house at the new I.C.I. chemical plant at Hillhouse. This modern works built close by the railway on farm land bordering the estuary became a strategic site in war time making noxious gases, one of the main products appeared to be phosgene gas, which could be a gas or a liquid and was highly volatile. It was also called Carbonyl Chloride. Used in making poisons, it could also be used in the making of dyes, resins and forms of plastic. In basic form it had been used effectively during the First World War. Ken's home was just a field and the width of the railway away from this dangerous works. The air was pungent much of the time. Ken's dad always ruled at home as fathers did back then and after the war when things were scarce, the harsh winter of 1947 hit people particularly hard. Fuel was in very short supply. The coal shed at 12 Hargate Road was looking quite empty so Ken arranged with his driver to drop a few big cobs of coal off the engine into the field by the house. Ken's driver Hughie Richmond, said *'We are not seeing your mother without coal, don't worry lad'.* They bailed the coal out under the cover of darkness and Ken waited until his dad had gone to work before he retrieved it, bagged it up, and placed it in the coal shed. Bert Bradshaw was spitting feathers when he saw it but Ken never let on where it had come from but of course the whole family knew. Having principles is one thing, keeping warm is quite another.

(left) From Burn Naze platform looking back towards Burn Naze South and Hilly Laid, the Hillhouse Works was on the left.

Departing from Thornton, we would have quickly passed Brown's coal yard on the left, the driver would have whistled for Hilly Laid Crossing and would continue accelerating as we travelled near Ken Bradshaw's house. The massive works complex at Hillhouse was on the right, seemingly busy and productive at all times. Along the right hand side all the way up to Burn Naze station and beyond, there were sidings, buildings, and pipe work leading to and from the many areas within the two works sites here, the Hillhouse chemical plant and the Ammonia Soda works at Burn Naze. There were numerous smaller chimneys, as well as those from the main boiler house, at both plants, emitting smoke or vapour and there were vapour trails floating skywards from various areas and pipe formations. There was quite often an unnatural odour in the air. Working conditions at both plants were very poor around the war years and just after. The chemical cocktails made at Hillhouse and the Salt extraction process at the Soda works left the workers both men and women in a sorry state of health. It was common to see workers exiting the plants at the end of a shift with their hair and clothing covered in a yellow powder. Few homes would have had a shower and instant hot water in the days when these factories were at the height of their production. Once we departed from Burn Naze station, we then began heading inland to skirt round the salt marshes for the run into Wyre Dock (see map on left). The original track formation when the railway was first built was straight along across the marshes on elevated trestle viaducts, embankments, etc; through to Dock Street in Fleetwood. Serious long term structural problems brought about a re-think as crossing the estuary in this manner had proved in time to be a bit too ambitious. On 10th August 1964, railcars 50778/50811 called at Burn Naze with 10am train from Blackpool North. **(below)** 'Lanky Bomber' **52857** of Wigan heads a Bamfurlong bound freight through Burn Naze. The buildings behind are the offices and distillation plant (tall structure) and also the boiler house and chimney for the waste heat boilers at the soda works. Pictures by *Chris Spring* and *C.A. Appleton*

BURN NAZE

AMMONIA WORKS

River Wyre

Burn Naze, 10th August 1964. We only made a brief stop at the little Halt at Burn Naze on our trip to Fleetwood, but it was long enough to gain a good idea of the surroundings by the station. Running into Burn Naze on the left side were rows of little terraced houses, the sort you would expect the see at fishing ports. Similar styles of housing could be seen locally at Fleetwood, Barrow and Morecambe. No doubt these small basic but comfortable little dwellings were placed here across from the works to cater for the large influx in the workforce which took place from the 1930's onwards. It is hard to describe, but entering Burn Naze station passing beneath the overbridge and coming to a stand, the design, the layout and the surrounding all seemed very austere, as if the station was just another part of the soda works. The fenced areas gave it all a prison camp effect I suppose. The map above only shows the ammonia soda works. The Hillhouse plant, nearer to Thornton, was even bigger and more complex. The ammonia soda works we see here processed salt that was pumped in brine form from the salt mines across the river Wyre at Preesall. The finished product of soda was in the form of powder or crystals and was used in detergents and cleaning agents for home use and in industry. Train loads of ammonia soda would leave Burn Naze daily for various parts of the country as the requirements dictated. The little platforms at Burn Naze halt could only accommodate four coaches yet in a morning the 8.4am businessman's train always called there with it's usual ten coach load on. In the 1950's, the I.C.I. built its own power station to supply all the needs of the factories and to sell any residue to the national grid. This power station was always referred to as Thornton power station. The CEGB built their own power plant on the reclaimed marshes at Wyre Dock around the same time. Leaving Burn Naze station behind and passing the Thornton power station on our left, we would have time to view the extent of the ammonia soda works over on the right side of the line (see drawing), which like the Hillhouse plant, always appeared to have plenty of work going on. It seemed ages before we left it behind, our little engine would be striding away steadily, the noise of the exhaust echoing between the buildings of the soda works that were nearest to the railway line. The land was quite open at this point and you could see at times right out to the river Wyre. The wind was often blowing and the breeze refreshing after the variety of smells we had just sampled. As we left the rows of sidings at the end of the plant, the main line curved ever more to the left as we began the run inland. More sidings could be seen here at Burn Naze North, which were filled as a rule with those top heavy Covhop wagons used for transporting the ammonia soda. The engine seen here is **84018** on the 10.25am Poulton –Fleetwood and the picture is by *Chris Spring*.

SODA

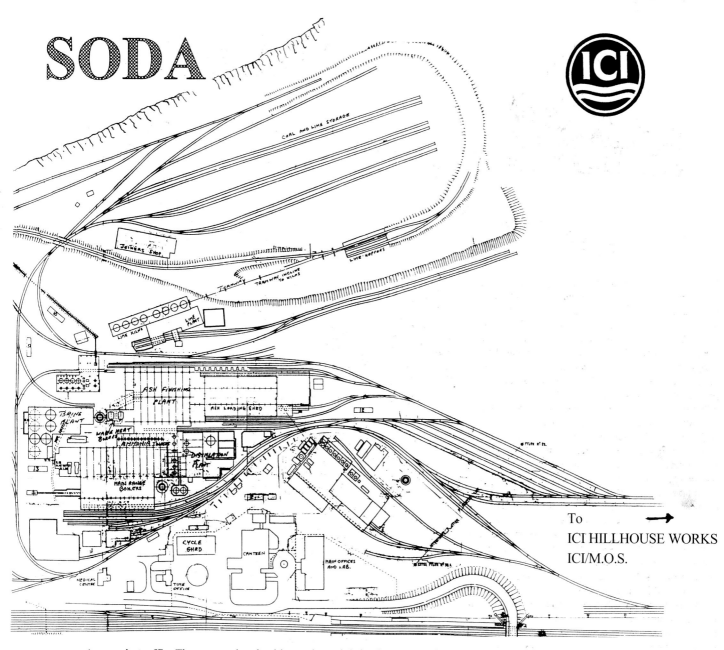

To
ICI HILLHOUSE WORKS
ICI/M.O.S.

Ammonia traffic. The process involved in turning salt brine into ammonia soda required large amounts of limestone being added and the substance then being heated and dried. Thousands of tons of coal came in to the works for this heating and drying process. High tonnages of limestone also arrived either by rail or by ship to the jetty on the river Wyre. Coal came by rail from the Wigan area and from

Yorkshire. The finished product, ammonia soda, would leave the works by the train load, either in bagged up form in open wagons, in box vans or in the hoppers, seen on the left. Ken Bradshaw worked these trains out of Burn Naze North around midnight, through to the Wembley area for Sudbury as part of Fleetwood turn 103. Archie Buchanan during his time at Willesden took them to Canning Town in the dockland area of London. Other trains went up the Barrow coast, like the one we see to the left with **42832** on the front (12/9/64). Gushetfoulds in the Glasgow area was another destination in later days.   Picture by *Chris Spring*

BURN NAZE
NORTH SIDINGS

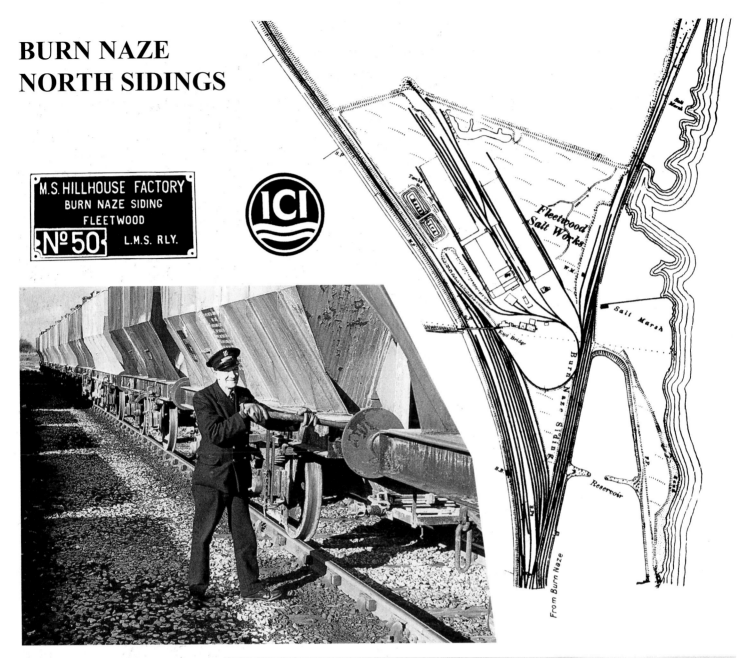

M.S. HILLHOUSE FACTORY
BURN NAZE SIDING
FLEETWOOD
Nº 50   L.M.S. RLY.

Shunting
at Burn Naze North

(above) Fleetwood guard Len Archer awaits his driver easing up on the coupling so he can flick the pole to knock the shackle off and split the wagons. Down at the business end (on the loco), driver Wilf Mann looks back as guard Archer pins down the brakes and makes ready for a shunt move to another road. This particular train is one of those bound for Gushetfoulds near Glasgow. The 'Covhop' wagons were deadly to work with when empty; they were very top heavy and when buffering up during shunting it was easy to get them buffer-locked. They were much more stable when fully loaded.   Pictures by *Tony Bretherton*

Early days at Wyre Power. It is 1955 and young Archie Buchanan, now a signalman, is covering the relief turn at the new Wyre Power station signal cabin on the edge of the salt marshes. Regular block coal train workings to the power station have yet to start. They were still testing which blends of coal were suitable for the burners. The load of coal coming in here is a special working, hence the Black Five on the front end. Burn Naze is right round the sweeping left hand curve, where we see the chimneys smoking in the top left of the picture. We are now almost at Wyre Dock and looking back towards Burn Naze and Thornton. The ammonia soda works chimneys are visible and the smoke seen behind the Burn Hall works (square building on the left skyline), may well be from the pile driving work taking place for the new Thornton (I.C.I.) power station. Pictures by *Archie Buchanan*

Fleetwood men. By the 1960's, Stanier Class 8F engines became more of a common sight around the Fylde, some replacing the Austerity 2-8-0's and the ageing 'Crab' 2-6-0's on the coal and soda ash workings. Others just visited on goods turns to Burn Naze and Wyre Dock. Driver Jack Preston, whose nickname was 'Marrow', eases **48618** off the shed at Wyre Dock Junction to run 'light' to Burn Naze North. The smiling young fireman is Tommy Dell.

Track plan labels: SCOTTISH RAILWAY, Marine Repairing Shop, Engine Shed, Returned Fish Box Yard, Conveyor to Fish Market, Ice Factory & Cold Store, FISH MARKET, FISH DOCK AREA 11 ACRES, Electric Coal Conveyors, S.B., RADCLIFFE ROAD, COPSE ROAD, Offices, 50 Ft. Wide, Swing Bridge, Slip, Slipways

WYRE DOCK JUNCTION

Fish, fish, and more fish. The sweeping right hand curve which skirted the salt marshes eased out into a long straight section close to Wyre Dock Junction. It was here where the motive power depot was to be found on the left hand side of the line and the marshalling yard and dock sidings were over to the right (see track plan above). As you reached Wyre Dock Junction, you suddenly became aware of just how important a fishing port Fleetwood was, even in the 1950's and into the early part of the 1960's. The whole area around by the fish dock was covered with sidings and railway wagons. Scores of fish vans, insulated fish vans and the like filled the extensive sidings. Over by the edge of the river Wyre were large coal sidings near the coal hoppers which filled the trawlers. The far side pilot would spend hours shunting here in the days before diesel powered boats took over. In the marshalling sidings near the main line, there was a lengthy cold store and ice making plant called the 'Ice House', which is still there today.

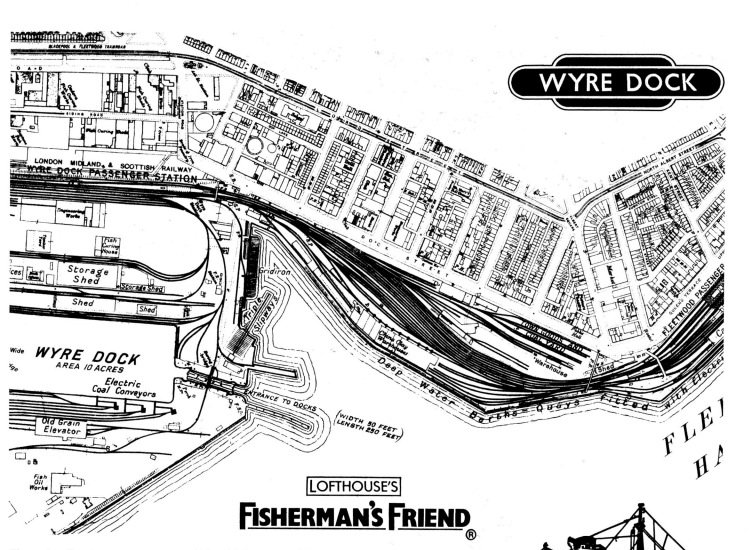

LOFTHOUSE'S
FISHERMAN'S FRIEND®

The push-pull trains seen over on page 118 and below are as follows; **(Opposite page-bottom left)** We see a very tidy 'Lanky' tank **50646** propelling the motor train into Fleetwood and passing the engine shed at Wyre Dock Junction (signal box seen far left) in April 1950. The other two pictures were taken by Tony Bretherton at the same spot some 15 years later in November 1965. They show (Opposite page-centre) 84010 driven by driver Wilf Mann, running into Wyre Dock, and coming out again in the view below. *Jim Davenport* took the picture of 50646.

FLEETWOOD LOCO

On shed at Fleetwood loco. As mentioned on page 117, The Stanier 'Big Eights' were quite common by the 1960's as we see here **(top left)**. Back in the 1940's, etc; things were much different in the motive power department. Coal trains from the Yorkshire coal fields and from yards at Wigan and Aintree would bring 'Austin Seven' and 'Lanky' Bomber 0-8-0's to Fleetwood. The Fowler 'Austin Sevens' were based at Rose Grove, Sowerby Bridge, Mirfield, Wigan, Aintree and Agecroft. Whilst they steamed like mad, in the motion department they were a disaster. They would tend to 'drop their guts', the inside motion would come down rendering them a complete failure. This usually happened when they had a lengthy string of wagons behind them, which really didn't help at all. In the early 1950's there were still a few 'Lanky' Bombers about. Springs Branch shed at Wigan had four of the big boilered types and Aintree depot had the rest, four big ones and five of the small boiler variety. **(above) 51419**, a 'Lanky' A class tank, was the relief far side pilot, Target No. 39 when seen here and finally, **84010** is acting as shed pilot, shunting the coal stage in a scene filmed by *Chris Spring* on the 16th December 1962.

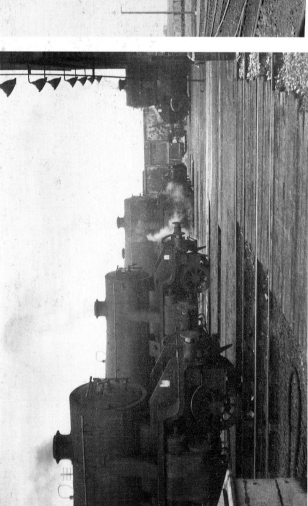

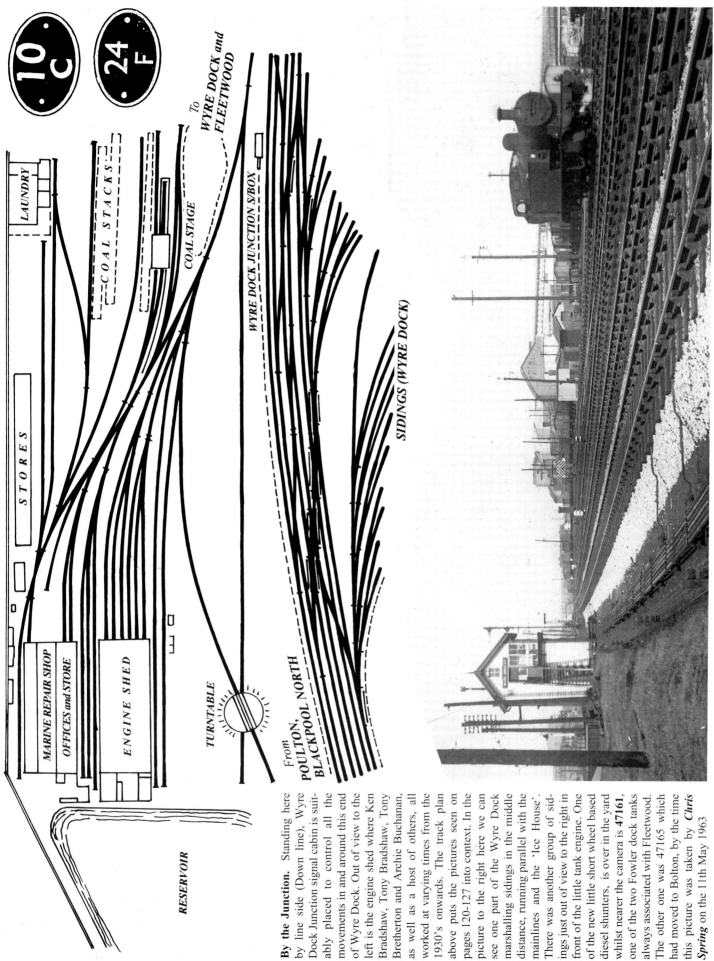

10 C   24 F

LAUNDRY

COAL STACKS

To WYRE DOCK and FLEETWOOD

S T O R E S

MARINE REPAIR SHOP

OFFICES and STORE

E N G I N E   S H E D

COAL STAGE

TURNTABLE

RESERVOIR

WYRE DOCK JUNCTION S/BOX

SIDINGS (WYRE DOCK)

From POULTON, BLACKPOOL NORTH

By the Junction. Standing here by line side (Down line), Wyre Dock Junction signal cabin is suitably placed to control all the movements in and around this end of Wyre Dock. Out of view to the left is the engine shed where Ken Bradshaw, Tony Bradshaw, Tony Bretherton and Archie Buchanan, as well as a host of others, all worked at varying times from the 1930's onwards. The track plan above puts the pictures seen on pages 120-127 into context. In the picture to the right here we can see one part of the Wyre Dock marshalling sidings in the middle distance, running parallel with the mainlines and the 'Ice House'. There was another group of sidings just out of view to the right in front of the little tank engine. One of the new little short wheel based diesel shunters, is over in the yard whilst nearer the camera is **47161**, one of the two Fowler dock tanks always associated with Fleetwood. The other one was 47165 which had moved to Bolton, by the time this picture was taken by *Chris Spring* on the 11th May 1963

Stored at Fleetwood. In April 1950, the two storage lines by the shed at Wyre Dock (Fleetwood) were occupied by half the depots complement of 'Lanky' tanks. Others were stored in the sidings situated between the loco shed and the marine works together with the odd 'A' class 0-6-0 tender engine. Blackpool's 'L&Y' tank engines were also out of use at the North shed. The arrival of the new Ivatt designed tank and tender engines had brought about the sudden demise of all but a handful of the old 'Lanky ' engines. As we saw on page 118, 50646 was almost ex-works and dashing about in 1950 on the motor trains, sister engine **50640,** seen to the left, was not that lucky. As Ken Bradshaw would be quick to point out, the new engines were fine provided the maintenance was good as well, but in those late 1940's and early 1950's, cleaning, repairs and looking after the engines somehow hit an all time low. The old 'Lanky' engines had been designed to keep going with very simple fitting care. The more modern designs with their niceties of rocking fire grates and hopper ash pans, as well as countless grease nipples instead of the simple oiling points meant you had to keep things greased on a regular basis. Stretched fitting staff often forgot about the greasing process. At washout periods, which tended to get extended causing boiler problems, back plate gauge glasses didn't get changed and would burst at times whilst the engine was in motion causing panic and confusion at the wrong time. The same storage roads which had held the 'Lanky' engines in the 1950's, played host to the stored Stanier Class 3 tanks from Blackpool in the period from 1961 to 1962 and 1963. **43502** (seen left), was stored at Fleetwood from December 1959 until July of 1962. Pictures by *Jim Davenport* and *Bert Holland*

End of the line

Stanier Class 3 tank No. **40109** proved to be the last one of these tidy looking engines to remain on the Fylde. As we can see it was in a sorry state by the 19th August 1962. It was probably the last to see use in the area along with 40164 which moved on to Lower Darwen at the back end of 1961. Why 40109 lasted longer than the others we don't know but it was in good order and low in mileage after its last visit to Horwich. It never really did anything in its last years. The engine made the long journey up to Airdrie in April 1963 to George Campbell's scrap yard. It is thought the engine seen in front of 40109 is 42434. **Picture by *Chris Spring***

Passing the shed

As we journeyed to Fleetwood in the years of 1961-62, I remember seeing these tank engines stored by the shed. It didn't register with me that these were the same little tank engines we had seen year after year shunting at Blackpool. They looked so weary, faded, grey and cold. It was the cab area I recall most of all. The view above of **40103** typifies just what I remember seeing, the cab windows were slid shut and grimy. You sensed their working days were over and felt as if they were from an era that had gone. 40103 was the first of the little Stanier's to go into store back in the summer of 1960. The scenes we see here were repeated on our excursion trips in the next couple of years. Engines in two's three's or even more would often be seen dumped amongst wagons in sidings waiting for their final appointment. **(right-centre) 40109** is seen again on the 16th December 1962, and **43502 (right-lower)** looks like it is welded to the track by rust as it sits near the buffers where it spent some two and a half years in store, this last picture being taken on 11th September 1961.

    Pictures by
    Chris Spring and ***Peter Fitton***

Changing shed scene. As pointed out, standards fell dramatically in post war years. Things were bad up to nationalisation, as the LMS, like other railway companies, was threadbare and cash strapped by the late 1940's. The 1950's brought a glimmer of hope but staff shortages in all departments caused serious operating problems, especially where maintenance was concerned. Ken Bradshaw (seen top left) had married in 1948 and in the early 1950's had two young children and was still working many weary night turns with little in the way of good wages to compensate for it. The night turns at Fleetwood in the 1950's included a number of empty wagon trains at periods through the night, starting with the 11/15pm to Aintree, the 11/55pm to Willesden (soda ash), 12.40am mixed goods to Collyhurst, 1/30am to Brindle Heath, 2/10am to Bamfurlong, 2/40am to Crofton (to Rose Grove) and at 4am another Wigan (Bamfurlong yard). When on nights on the shed Ken would arrange with the fitting staff to put his car in the marine works over the pit that fitters used for locomotives, 40109 is standing on the same pit in 1963 having the motion stripped down. Ken had in later years exchanged his motor bikes for a little sports car; it was a 1936 Singer 'Le Manns' which he found sheeted up awaiting repair at the back of the garage at Four Lane Ends–not far from George Formby's house now called Kirkstiles. Once repaired and tuned up it really could leave others standing. **(above)** 76087 is parked up ready to work the 5/30pm fish train to Marple. Pictures by **Ken Bradshaw, Chris Spring** and **Tony Bretherton**

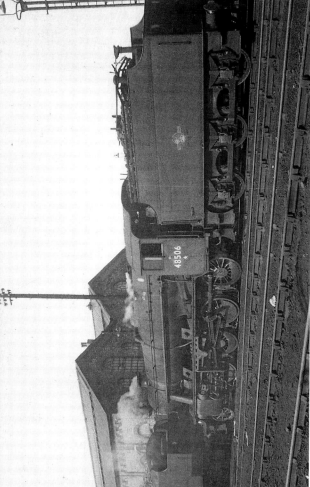

'FLEETWOOD LOCO'

Days of grime. Little in the way of cleaning was done as time went on. Cleaners would often be used as labourers helping the fitting staff, boilersmiths, etc., The young lads didn't complain as the pay was better on labouring rates. Then before you knew it you were out firing, covering sickness and holidays, etc., **(above)** The gang of men seen by the little mess hut, facing into the sun are, fitter Eddy Colley, a young hand cleaner, then driver, Wilf Mann and fireman Chris Doyle. The date is thought to be October 1964. The engines seen here are **48506** by the marine works and over on the shed roads we have **42960** and **42844** as well as **84017**.

Pictures by *Tony Bretherton* and *Stuart Taylor*

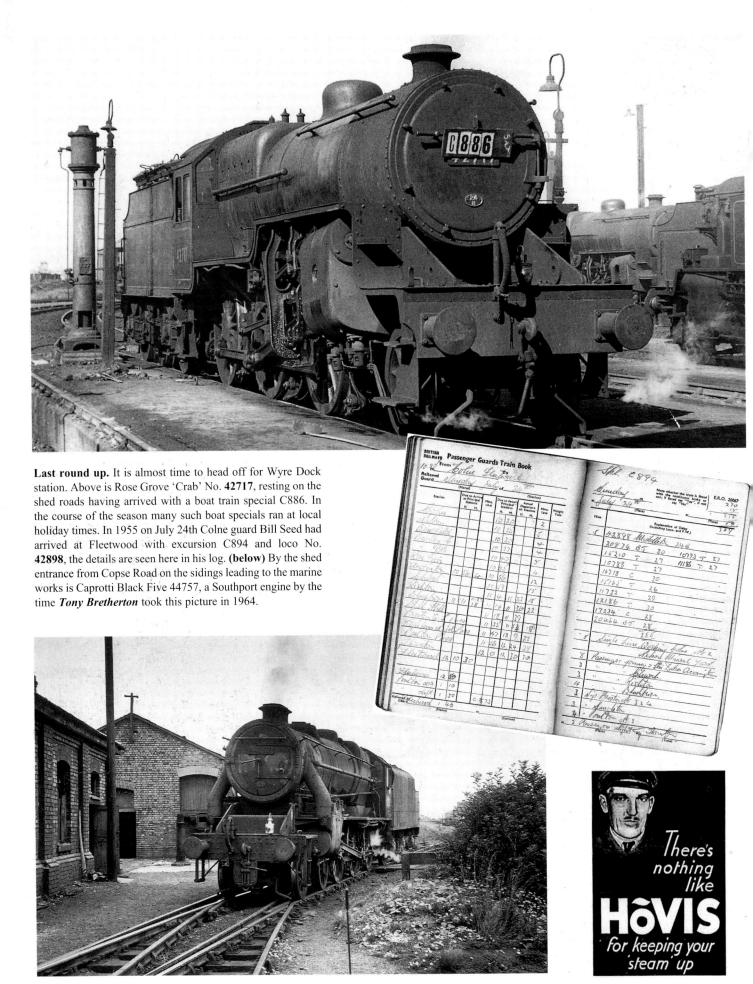

Last round up. It is almost time to head off for Wyre Dock station. Above is Rose Grove 'Crab' No. **42717**, resting on the shed roads having arrived with a boat train special C886. In the course of the season many such boat specials ran at local holiday times. In 1955 on July 24th Colne guard Bill Seed had arrived at Fleetwood with excursion C894 and loco No. **42898**, the details are seen here in his log. **(below)** By the shed entrance from Copse Road on the sidings leading to the marine works is Caprotti Black Five 44757, a Southport engine by the time *Tony Bretherton* took this picture in 1964.

Passing by. Time to go, one last look, sees 'WD' 2-8-0 No. **90164** by the coal stage on 11th May 1963. Peter Fitton took the picture and Frank Dean was by his side doing just the same. **(below)** A scene from the carriage as we leave the shed behind. Tidy BR Standard Class 2 tank No. **84010** is shunting. Six of these little tank engines came to Fleetwood eventually, they were 84010/11/12/16/17/18. Numbers 84010 and 84016 stayed until 1965, then they went to Lostock Hall for storage prior to going to Crewe for overhaul for use on the Isle of Wight; this sadly never happened. Numbers 84012 and 84017 left in 1963 for Southport but 'No' 12 was cut up soon after. The last two at Fleetwood were 84011 and 84018 (another Isle of Wight candidate), which were withdrawn in April 1965. Pictures by *Peter Fitton*

'WHEEZY' ANNA'S

Dock shunts. As well as the 'A' class saddle tanks, Fleetwood kept two of the Fowler dock tanks right up to 1962. **47161** and **47165** were always the pair. The beginning of the 1960's saw the little 170hp diesel shunters arrive on the scene and they would eventually oust the old Fowler engines out of their regular shunt turns at Wyre Dock. 47161 stayed on as a stand-by but 47165 migrated to Bolton, going to Horwich works for repair. It never came back and stayed at Bolton till 1964, where the men nicknamed it the 'rocking horse'; Fleetwood men called them 'Wheezy Anna's'. When Ken Bradshaw was on the night shunts he would take it in turns with his driver Hughie Richmond to have the night off. Hughie would say, *'Ken, there's a good picture on at the cinema tonight .....Can you manage ?'*.... and Ken would say *'Aye, off you go, I'll have tomorrow off'*. **(left)** Driver Len Payne sits on loco. **70018** whilst working the 2/50 fish. Pictures by *Peter Fitton* and *Tony Bretherton*

The 2/50 fish to Broad Street. The one turn at Fleetwood which everyone remembers is the afternoon fish train from Wyre Dock that Fleetwood men at one time worked through to Willesden and then lodged. Ken Bradshaw did just that in the war years and just after when the load was always 52 vans of fish. By the late 1940's and early 1950's, the job had altered and the men only worked it to Crewe. Here the train was split up and sent in different directions. Archie Buchanan, then a fireman at Willesden, would relieve his former work mates at Crewe, having lodged. There were two more big fish trains to Broad Street, which ran at 7pm and at 10pm, the latter running as required though. The motive power in the 1940's and 1950's was usually express power in the shape of Royal Scot class engines (both types), Patriots (both types) and 5X's. The locomotives generally were Crewe engines which worked into Blackpool North with a overnight parcels then took the boat train round to Fleetwood tender first and then sat on the shed till the afternoon. This was a 'running-in' turn at one time.

Later days on the 2/50 fish. On the day Tony Bretherton was firing the fish train, he took these pictures of his mate driver Len Payne and the engine before departure. 'Britannia' No. **70018**, *Flying Dutchman* was on the job that day. By 1964 the writing was on the wall for this type of fish traffic by rail. The Beeching regime had declared that there would be an end to the carrying of perishables by rail. Local railway bosses advised the fish traders at Fleetwood that in future only one train a day would leave the port and only go as far as Crewe. The railway management informed the fishermen that if they wanted anything else, they would have to make there own arrangements ….. So they did. They quickly formed the Fleetwood Fish Transport Company using their own refrigerated road vehicles and that was the end of fish traffic by rail as far as Fleetwood was concerned. Wyre Dock declined and Fleetwood loco shed closed two years later and would in time become a coal concentration depot.

Leaving Wyre Dock Junction

Jim Turner is now our driver into Fleetwood. He is seen here in the cab of our little train engine, one of the 84XXX Class engines. As we leave Wyre Dock Junction behind and travel along the straight by the 'Ice House' towards Wyre Dock station, we will see the 'A' Class tanks in action. Much of the 1940's and just into the 1950's, Wyre Dock marshalling yard had a familiar member of female staff. It was of course 'Tiger' the tabby cat. Every one knew her and in her 12 years on the docks, it is a safe bet to say she lost a fair few of her nine lives. Sadly, she was accidentally poisoned and was cremated in the firebox of engine No. **51321** (seen on the right). There were usually three 'A' Class tank engines at work in the yards by the main line all through the 1950's. 51376, 51477, and 51498 covered the early 1950's and 51321 then joined them and 51498 left to go to Lower Darwen. 51336 came and 51321 was withdrawn in February 1958. By 1960, 51336, 51419 and 51524 were still at work, but only 51419 survived to 1961, being withdrawn in September of that year. Jim Turner picture by **Tony Bretherton**

Attaching a portion

The short term replacement for the old 'A' Class tank engines came in the form of the Fowler No. 3 shunt engines which really had the bleakest of cabs, not the best machines on which to spend a shift. The engine back plate wasn't lagged and with the constant backwards, then forwards, movement of shunting, together with the 'rough shunt moves', hitting wagons up, then there was every danger of sticking your hand by accident on the bare firebox back and getting burnt. Wearing gloves was a sensible option here. **47666** is on Target 94 and is sitting in the loop near Wyre Dock Junction cabin, as a train bound for Manchester pauses to attach a fish van on the rear and to change crews. The relief guard can be seen making his way to the rear to where the shunter is stood waiting for the van load of fish to be buffered up on the rear end. Picture by *Bert Holland*

Shunt turns at Fleetwood. The were a number of shunting turns in the days when Wyre Dock was still a busy fishing port, most of these Target jobs lasting until the early 1960's. In the 1950's however, quite a lot of the shunting work was made into just two shifts, the night turns no longer being required. Target 36 was the Fleetwood and Wyre Dock pilot, No. 37 was called the 'Junction Drummer' and this turn shunted all the arrivals in the sidings using the lengthy head shunts. No. 38 was the far side pilot shunting the grain sidings and the coal hopper roads over by the estuary side. Target No. 40 made up the fish trains and vacuum tested them ready for the train engine to simply back up and blow-up. Other targets shunted the other end of Wyre Dock, the timber sidings and the clay warehouse, etc., **(right) 51336,** just a month away from withdrawal, shunts at Wyre Dock on 15th October 1960. Picture by *Chris Spring.*

MANX KIPPERS

The best to you **FROM FLEETWOOD**

Wyre Dock station. Our last calling point before reaching Fleetwood was here at Wyre Dock's island platform. It had been a short straight run along from the shed at Wyre Dock Junction. Industry abounded on the left as we approached the station. All of it related to the fish trade. There were processing factories and kipper smoking plants and the air was full of the smell of fish products. It really was a cats dream of heaven. Over on the right side of the line we would run along by the lengthy marshalling yard sidings and the docks buildings which included the 'Ice House' with it's conveyer belt runways over to the docks that took the ice blocks down to the trawlers. Nearer to Wyre Dock station, there was quite a large wood storage yard within the docks. Approaching the platform, the breeze seemed to get stronger, the view began to open up and we gained our first look out across the estuary, a scene which would get better once we departed for Fleetwood. Seagulls circled noisily above us eagerly looking for any bits of fish that may be on offer around the docks. **84016** is the engine seen here working the Fleetwood portion of the 1/40pm from Manchester on the 11th May 1963. Picture by *Chris Spring*

Making for Fleetwood

The view on the right of the DMU is very similar to what we would see as we departed the platform. Passengers would make their way off the platform via the walkway and then the footbridge over to Dock Street. **(below)** The docks complex at Wyre Dock is seen to best effect in this view taken from the air. The fish dock is seen nearest with Wyre Dock beyond. The railway station is in the top left of the picture, with the 'Ice House' just visible down the left side. The fish warehouses run round the edge of the docks and over to the right, in the area known as the far side, are the coal hoppers and sidings for the trawlers and also the huge grain storage silo over by the side of the estuary.

Railcar picture by *Chris Spring.*

WYRE DOCK

That busy crossing. Leaving Wyre Dock station is probably one of my best memories of the run to Fleetwood. There was an air of excitement as Wyre Dock was left behind, suddenly after being 'en-route' as it were, we felt we had arrived at Fleetwood, well not quite, but it certainly felt like it. It really felt that way back in the 1950's when we were young and very impressionable. The level crossing here was always busy, lots of road wagons would be going to and from the docks as well as vans and pick up trucks. Over in Dock Street itself and by Station Road, lorries and cars, etc., always filled the road to some extent. In Dock Street, suppliers to the fish trade, The Coal Salt and Tanning Company had it's offices and warehouses. They are seen in the top left of this view and they appeared to have taken over most of the buildings along the street at this point. It was still about a mile into the terminus at Fleetwood and after leaving the crossing seen here, the lines took sweeping curves, first to the right towards the wide expanse of the river, then curving inland to the left to run along the edge of the deep water dock into the station by the landing stage. As enginemen would say, **840, - 18.** one of the little Standard tanks quickly runs into Wyre Dock from Fleetwood on Saturday 10th August 1964 with the 11.25am Fleetwood to Kirkham service. 84018 was one of those engines earmarked to go to the Isle Of Wight between 1965 and 1966 but sadly the project was abandoned in favour of electrification and the use of old underground stock from London Transport. Picture by *Chris Spring*

On the Gridiron. It was the summer of 1944 when this view was taken, the allies have already invaded Europe and the fight to end the Second World War was looking good. Meanwhile, here on the docks at Fleetwood, the old wooden Gridiron is being replaced with concrete. Wyre Dock station is up above us out of view behind the Gourock Rope Works building. The level crossing is just above the boats we see marooned on the Grid and Dock Street lies beyond the railway, it's buildings hidden by the warehouse in the top right of the picture.

WYRE DOCK STATION

STAFF ONLY

What a view ! This has to rank as my favourite scene in the book and it portrays my most vivid memory of the outing by rail to Fleetwood..... that of leaving Wyre Dock station and seeing out across the expanse of water in the Wyre estuary. Our little tank engine would noisily ease out of the station here its exhaust would echo against the buildings on Dock Street and on days when the sky was blue and somewhat cloudless, then the rising exhaust from the chimney would drift, carried on the wind skywards but also out towards the estuary, billowing white clouds would float towards the boats that bobbed about at their moorings in the deep water dock. The seagulls would be circling around in large numbers 'shouting the odds', ever looking for a free meal and fighting when they did. Looking out intensely and excited we would scan the estuary and the distant shore, which seemed so far away when we were young. With a steady 'bark', our engine would purposefully head off towards Fleetwood curving away to the right leaving the hustle and bustle of Dock Street. In the view above, the sidings to the right of the train provide lengthy storage for vans and coaching stock whilst the warehouse on the right was known as the clay shed. Picture by *Chris Spring*

Dock Street on Market day. When the Fleetwood Arms Hotel was having its frontage repaired, this busy scene was taken from the scaffolding. The pavement here by Preston Street, still juts out further than on the rest of Dock Street even today, though you will never witness scenes like this ever again. Somewhere in the region of fifty "Chara's,, (charabanc/coaches) are parked up here and way into the distance up to Queens Terrace. In the region of 2000 visitors had arrived on these coaches and would be all walking in cramped style round the indoor and outdoor markets and filling up just about all the seats in the local

cafes and tea rooms. Add to these figures the numbers of people visiting Fleetwood on holiday by car and train and it is easy to see why the town did so well in the years up to the 1970's. The carriage sidings on the right would easily hold 15 plus coaches -see this area from the air on page 154. On the run into Fleetwood one day, Ken Bradshaw and his mate hit two platelayers on the curves leading into the station area. The wind was biting and the trackmen simply never heard Ken coming. The first Ken knew about it was when they were met at the buffers in Fleetwood station and asked to examine their engine, When the big Icelandic trawlers

sailed into Fleetwood their hefty crew members set about buying up the town, stocking up on supplies as well as visiting the pubs and the local ladies of the night. As Ken shunted carriages in the sidings by Dock Street one morning, a bedroom shutter went up on a house across in Dock Street. A tirade of abuse was followed by the sight of a seaman toppling out of the window onto the pavement below. He simply picked himself up and staggered along to the Fleetwood Arms Hotel for another skin full !...........
Picture from the archive of *Lighthouse Stationary, North Albert Street, Fleetwood*

On the run in

We are now on the final stretch, with the lengthy platforms of Fleetwood station just a short distance away. **(above)** This view looks out across the deep water dock area towards the salt marshes and was taken in 1962 from the footbridge, which is visible in the picture seen below to the right. The railway company dredger is tied up at its moorings, and on quiet days when this machine was hard at work, the sound of it pumping away could be heard all over the town. Driver Tony Bradshaw (above right), has finished oiling round **84010** and is about to rejoin the comparative comfort of the warm cab before leaving Dock Street yard with the coaching stock of yet another local train. Taken from the footbridge that spanned the platform ends at Fleetwood, we can see the station signal box, the footbridge leading onto the quay side and over to the right the goods warehouse at the end of Dock Street. In the distance is the Wyre Power station on the salt marshes on the edge of the river Wyre. Pictures by *Tony Bretherton* and *Stuart Taylor*

FLEETWOOD STATION

On the locals

(below) **40164**, the little Stanier tank engine seen here looks in fine fettle in this Spring 1961 view. It is more than likely this locomotive, was the last of the type to see service locally though 40109 was also steamable at that time. The engine along with the others of the class formerly based at Blackpool had moved to Fleetwood as spare engines and for storage as we saw earlier. The Indian summer (or was it spring) at Fleetwood was soon over and 40164 moved on to Blackburn with 40072, but by the back end of 1962 she was standing on the scrap roads at Horwich works, with the remains of the poppet valve 'Crabs' behind her.

FLEETWOOD

The station approaches

It was quite a tightly curved angle of entry into the platforms at Fleetwood. Despite the lack of view, enginemen, shunters and the like quite happily backed trains of fifteen coaches in length in and out of the station. The long dock side platform could easily accommodate trains of this length that ran in connection with the Isle of Man boats. The dredger on the landing stage was operated by the railway marine department, whose staff monitered the river and the constantly changing channels. What memories this view must bring back for enginemen like Ken Bradshaw, approaching the station would often mean the end of another shift was in sight. It was at this point as our train braked for the platform edge that we took a last look out to sea and breathed in the salty air, before gathering up our belongings ready for that dash to the market.

Dock Street goods. As we can see, wagons are still being shunted into the warehouse here in July 1962 and house hold coal is still very much a day to day commodity. The local coal merchants lorry looks weighed down as it eases out of the yard. I well remember curving round by the goods shed here, on our journeys into Fleetwood. The walls of the goods shed seemed so close you could touch them. Pictures by *Stuart Taylor*

Journey's end

The little tank engine which had brought us to Fleetwood slipped quietly into the platform and the large carriage wheels made a ringing noise as they took the curve at the platform end. Most times the weather was bright and clear, even sunny on some occasions. Out across the estuary towards the sea, the water looked murky and the breeze was decidedly salty but always fresh. The smell of fish was evident or was it fish meal ?… Over to the left there was a restricted view of the houses in Queen's Terrace, which ran all along side of the station. The houses always looked rather regal and somewhat Victorian. There was excitement and a feel of adventure, especially in our younger days as we jumped out of the compartment and slammed the carriage door shut, before joining the rest of the crowd making for the barrier some distance away deep in the bowels of the station. Dad in his usual military manner was striding ahead with mum straining to keep up and brother Bert and I would be trotting along in fine fashion taking in everything around us. Who would have thought that between 40 and 50 years later, I would be recalling these annual events of another life time. The journey from Blackpool had taken about 30 minutes and covered just nine miles but it certainly left a lasting impression on me.

Pictures by *Stuart Taylor*

FLEETWOOD

ISLE OF MAN

MADDOX

BRITISH RAILWAYS

Busy days by the sea. Giving the impression of high season traffic, the stored carriages by the quay side makes you wonder if the Isle of Man TT races are on. Things were always hectic with special boat trains and the like at these times. The boats would be full to capacity and the station would be constantly crowded with passengers either going to the Isle of Man or coming back. Things continued that way right through to the late 1950's. In the summer of 1952, Ivatt tank No. **41281** sits in the short bays on the left, waiting to go to Kirkham and Wesham. Black Five No. **44895,** standing on Platform 4, is going to Manchester Victoria. Over to the right, **84016** is being stoked up ready for a trip to Blackpool North.

Station scenes. Ginger haired driver Jim Hornby, with those sparkling eyes of his, poses with his hand on the brake handle for his fireman that day Tony Bretherton. Over on page 142 at the top, we see Ivatt tank engine No. **41260** in number one platform with the houses in Queen's Terrace behind. The short bays, numbered 2 and 3, are nearer the camera. (**Left**, page 142) the parachute tank at the platform end proved very useful even for engines heading for the shed. It was handy to quickly top up the tank just in case there was a queue when you got back. Jim Hornby picture by **Tony Bretherton**

FLEETWOOD

Resting in the No. 3 bay platform (short bay) at Fleetwood is Ken Bradshaw's favourite Black Five 4-6-0 of the early 1950's, No. **45214**. This engine together with sister engine No. 45212, had come to Fleetwood in the late 1940's from Bradford's Low Moor depot. Ken worked many a boat train special with both these engines in the years after the war. In Ken's famous little snap shot, the one we have seen in this book a couple of times, his driver Hughie Richmond got Ken to pose for him as they waited at Fleetwood to work a 15 coach boat train special taking internees who had come back from the Isle of Man to Crewe on their way back to their respective homes. Whilst 45212 stayed fairly local, the furthest it moved was to Carlisle, 45214 would for some reason end up on the Scottish Region. The move in the mid 1950's took her to Stirling where she stayed for the rest of her working life. 45212 outlived her sister, going on to work right up to the last day of steam. Working the last steam hauled train to Blackpool South, then performing the last normal move of a steam engine on B.R., shunting the sleeping cars in Preston station and the engine still survives today. Both these Black Fives were noted as being very strong engines for their class. **(left) 42296** stands on No. 4 platform with the 9.55am working to Kirkham on 10th August 1964. This was just about a month after our last ever visit by rail to Fleetwood. Pictures here **Stuart Taylor collection and Chris Spring**

FLEETWOOD

Saturday 6th July

THORNTON CLEVELEYS — FLEETWOOD

FROM	Schedule Nos.		163	162	52	RETURN FARES SECOND CLASS — Thornton Cleveleys	Fleetwood
		TIMES OF DEPARTURE				s d	s d
		a m	a m	a m	a m		
EARBY	…	6B 59	—	—	—	15/10	17/-
FOULRIDGE	…	7B 6	—	—	—	14/10	16/-
COLNE	…	—	—	—	—	—	15/6
NELSON	…	—	7 5	—	—	—	14/10
BRIERFIELD	…	—	7 11	—	8 16	13/6	14/6
BURNLEY CENTRAL	…	—	7 16	—	8 16	13/-	13/6
BURNLEY BARRACKS	…	—	7 22	—	8 19	12/4	13/6
ROSE GROVE	…	—	7 32	7 0	8 25	12/4	13/4
PADIHAM	…	—	—	7 7	8 28	12/-	13/-
HAPTON	…	—	—	7 10	8 33	—	13/-
SIMONSTONE	…	—	—	7 13	—	—	12/8
THORNTON CLEVELEYS … arr.		a m 9 33	8 51	—	9 54		
FLEETWOOD … ,,		9 45	—	8 27	10 0		

B—Change at Burnley Central and Preston

ADDITIONAL RETURN SERVICES—SATURDAY 13th JULY
FLEETWOOD depart 10‡15 a.m., 11.40 a.m., 1.10 p.m., 7.30 p.m. to PADIHAM, ROSE GROVE and stations to COLNE.
‡ Calls Thornton Cleveleys 10.24 a.m.

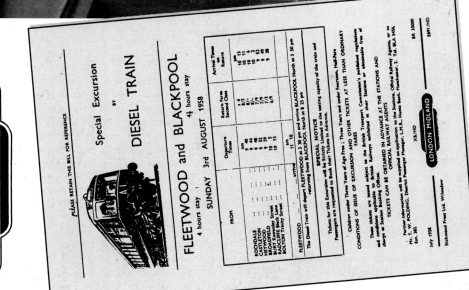

PLEASE RETAIN THIS BILL FOR REFERENCE

Special Excursion
BY
DIESEL TRAIN

FLEETWOOD and BLACKPOOL
4 hours stay   4½ hours stay

SUNDAY 3rd AUGUST 1958

FROM	Departure Times	Return Fares Second Class	Arrival Times on Return
ROCHDALE			
CASTLETON			
HEYWOOD			
BROADFIELD			
BURY Knowsley Street			
BURY Loco Back Lane			
RADCLIFFE Black Lane			
BOLTON Trinity Street	11 10		

The Diesel Train will depart FLEETWOOD at 2.30 pm and arrive BLACKPOOL North at 3 50 pm ; returning from BLACKPOOL North at 8 25 pm

SPECIAL NOTICE

The Diesel Train will be Strictly Limited to the seating capacity of the train and Passengers are requested to Book their Tickets in Advance.

Tickets for this Excursion will be Strictly Limited

CONDITIONS OF ISSUE OF EXCURSION FARES

Children under Three Years of Age Free ; Three Years and under Fourteen, Half-Fare

These tickets are issued subject to the British Transport Commission's published regulations and conditions applicable to British Railways exhibited at their Stations or obtainable free of charge at Station Booking Offices.

TICKETS CAN BE OBTAINED IN ADVANCE AT THE STATIONS AND OFFICIAL RAILWAY AGENTS

Further information will be supplied on application to the Stations, Official Railway Agents, or to Mr. T. W. FOLDING, District Passenger Manager, L.M.R., Hunts Bank, Manchester, 3. Tel. BLA 345A.

July 1958

Richmond Press Ltd. Wilmslow

LONDON MIDLAND

BR 35000
E69/HD
X8/HD

Fleetwood – Platform Four

Platform numbers one and four both ran beneath the train shed roof right up to the concourse area. The short bays which stopped short of the train shed were numbered two and three. The station offices and Booking Hall, etc., were to be found running down the middle of the station as we see here all the main buildings were to the left of platform No. 4. If you kept walking down here along the platform you would find the ticket barriers at the end and a slope leading up thereafter onto the main concourse. Sadly, as this view shows, Fleetwood station became in its last years quite rundown and neglected in appearance.

9/55am departure. (left) Another view of **42296** on 10th august 1964, this time taken by Tony Bretherton, I wonder if he was the fireman that day ?.....this picture also shows us the boat train platform number five, which handled the longest trains that used Fleetwood station.

(below) Close by at the ticket barrier, the sun is streaming down and there are few passengers about. The station from the edge of the platforms up to and including the concourse had wooden flooring. The dry, dusty boards gave the building a very hollow sound as countless pairs of feet, all tramping about, generated a fair degree of noise. As we reached the barrier, dad would be ready with the Runabout Rover tickets, holding them out in a fan, the way he had done at Blackpool. We would be ushered through the wooden gate and on up the slope, our feet tapping out a tune on the lengthy wooden floor boards. Straight ahead of us, across the concourse, the clatter of china cups and the smell of warm cooking was evident from the refreshment rooms, the same ones Ken Bradshaw always referred to as the 'Refresh'.

Making for the streets. (below-Page 147) Looking at those two lads by the barrier on Platform No. 1, it could almost be me and brother Bert making our way off and up the wooden decking slope onto the concourse. The sun is shining bright on this occasion. Sadly, on our last outing by rail to Fleetwood, in that poor summer of 1964, we passed through the station here dodging the puddles before making a dash between showers down to the market. In the sunny years, though walking up onto the concourse at Fleetwood was a pleasure, children would be running about, the noise of prams running over the floor boards was present and there was laughter and excitement in the air. Over to the right as we briefly stood on the concourse you would see the archway leading out to the jetty through which passengers heading for the Isle of Man boats would walk. The refreshment rooms were along the end wall of the station and always seemed to be doing a fair trade. To our left was another large archway which took you out onto Queen's Terrace, (the main entrance). Out there on the street, the sunlight would be very bright indeed on occasions and as we headed out of that main entrance we would often wince as the bright light hit us full on. Just outside on the front there, things were usually hectic, there would be large crowds of holidaymakers milling around. Buses pulling in by the station and over by the ferry terminal we would see the trams resting before setting off back to Blackpool. Happy days indeed.

DOUGLAS Isle of Man
Via FLEETWOOD and the ISLE OF MAN STEAM PACKET COMPANY'S STEAMERS

Friday Night & Saturday 5th & 6th July

STATION MASTER

Station staff. The picture above is a Coronation 'get together' of Fleetwood station staff. The picture is taken on the concourse with the slope up from No. 1 platform on the left and the main archway out onto Queen's Terrace visible in the right background. The staff are as follows, on the back row, left to right, we have Porter B Brace; Ticket Collector C Greaves; Guard Jack Cookson; Porter/Guard J Thompson; Parcels Porter B Anyon; Porter M McCleod; the chap in the beret is the station fitter (C&W). On the front row we have Station Foreman D Radcliff; Mr. Kemp the District Block Inspector; Mr. Davis the Station Master; J Lupton, Station Clerk and T Hodgson, Station Inspector.

Picture by *Jack Cookson*

BRITISH RAILWAYS
STEAMERS

FROM	Through Trains to Fleetwood					RETURN FARES		
	Friday 5th July	Saturday 6th July				1st Class through-out	2nd Class Rail and 1st Class Steamer	2nd Class through-out
Schedule Nos.	160	—	163	162	52			
	p m	a m	a m	a m	a m	s d	s d	s d
EARBY	10C 2	6B 59	—	—	—	82/-	73/6	63/6
FOULRIDGE	10C 9	7B 6	—	—	—	80/6	72/6	62/6
COLNE	10 25	—	7 5	—	—	79/10	72/-	62/-
NELSON	10 32	—	7 11	—	R 16	78/10	71/4	61/4
BRIERFIELD	10 37	—	7 16	—	8 19	78/4	71/-	61/-
BURNLEY CENTRAL	10 45	—	7 22	7 0	8 25	76/10	70/-	60/-
BURNLEY BARRACKS	10 50	—	—	7 2	8 28	76/10	70/-	60/-
ROSE GROVE	10 55	—	—	7 7	8 33	76/6	69/10	59/10
PADIHAM	11 2	—	—	7 10	—	76/-	69/6	59/6
HAPTON	—	—	7 32	—	—	76/-	69/6	59/6
SIMONSTONE	11 8	—	—	7 13	—	75/6	69/2	59/2

FLEETWOOD arrive	a m 12 18	a m 9 45	a m 8 51	a m 8 26	a m 10 0
FLEETWOOD Steamer depart	a m 1 30	10 30			
DOUGLAS arrive	6 0	1 0 pm			

B—Change at Burnley Central and Preston
C—Change at Colne

Passengers RETURN from DOUGLAS any weekday within three months, including date of issue (for time of sailing see Steamship Company's announcement), proceeding from FLEETWOOD by ANY Ordinary Train having a through connection. On Saturday 13th July, Through Return Service from Douglas Steamer and Rail will operate as follows :—

Douglas Steamer depart	a m 6 30	a m 7 30	a m 8 30	p m 4 0
Fleetwood Steamer approx arrive	9 30	10 30	11 30	7 0
Fleetwood Through Train depart	10 15	11 40	p m 1 10	7 30

To Padiham, Rose Grove, Burnley Barracks and Central and Brierfield, Nelson and Colne

The Passenger Station at Fleetwood adjoins the Quay, and enables passengers and their luggage to pass direct from the train to the steamer, and NO EXPENSE is incurred by this route in the transfer of luggage to or from the steamer.

By the 'Refresh'. If we looked to our right as we walked across the concourse, this is the view we would have, showing the refreshment rooms and on the far right the archway leading down to the landing stage is just visible. Outside on the slope down to the steamers there was a wooden ticket hut manned for years by Fred Brown. If you recall this is the 'Refresh' into which a young Ken Bradshaw dashed the day he stuck the coal pick though driver Swarbrick's tea bottle, luckily the girls were able to help him out. Note the L & Y and LNWR notice on the wall of the concourse, still visible in the summer of 1960, in this view by **Ken Roberts**

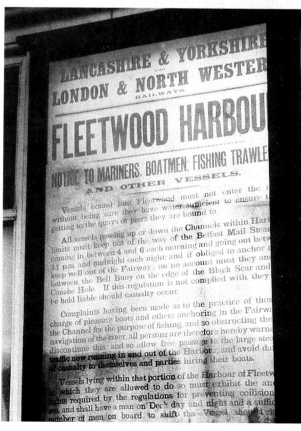

Out on to Queen's Terrace

(right) The frontage of Fleetwood station looks quiet in this picture. The scene was very different in the 1950's, especially at the height of the summer season. The sheer size and proportions of the station indicate that it was clearly built to handle large volumes of passengers, and it did so, quite adequately for a great many years. The main building here was faced with cream and red glazed bricks and they always remained quite clean in the sea air elements. Stations with similar brickwork in the Lancashire mill towns were often blackened and covered in grime. Note the canopies over the footpath along the station wall; these were provided by the Manx Government as shelter for passengers queuing for the Isle of Man boats.

Picture by Tony Bretherton

Catching the tram

Well, we haven't visited the market yet, but this is where we would catch the tram later in the day for a ride all the way to Blackpool's South Shore and the Pleasure Beach. An early afternoon tea was usually consumed after our visit to the market in one of the café's somewhere up near the Pharos's lighthouse. It would be one of the traditional old cafes with net curtains at the windows, gingham table cloths and nippy waitresses. Along here by the Ferry terminal (see left), there were a number of little trinket shops, the odd café and of course the famous fishmongers where you could get your Manx kippers sent to your home address.

Along Queen's Terrace. Here we are by the station. It is alongside here that we would usually walk to the market. To us, back in the 1950's, the houses along Queen's Terrace looked quite grand. In this view though, they are out of sight to the left of the picture. As we see, the road is very wide, allowing ample parking for the many cars which now appear to have arrived on the scene in those early post war years bordering the 1950's. It would be in the early part of the 1950's when the steamer services to the Isle of Man went back to being as busy as they were back in the 1930's. In the height of the season and around the time of the 'TT' races, droves of people would come by train and queue six deep out along the pavement here on Queen's Terrace by the wall side of the station waiting for the next available boat to the Isle of Man. Sometimes up to three boats would be booked to leave within minutes of each other to cope with the mass of people waiting at the Fleetwood landing stage. At the busiest times the boats simply ran a shuttle service back and forwards to the island until the backlog of passenger was cleared. The captains of these boats often took calculated gambles with the tides to get in and out of the narrow channel leading into the deep water dock. It wasn't uncommon for one of the big boats to scrape its hull whilst traversing the silted up channel. By 1951, passenger complaints about waiting out in the open with no protection from the weather had reached an all time high. The Manx Government funded the construction of a lengthy lean-to awning that ran along the train shed wall covering a fair length of the pavement along Queen's Terrace. It is visible in the later years pictures of the station and as the bus stops are at that point, it was easy to think the awning was placed their for their passengers benefit, not so. The new awning was built in time for the summer 1952 sailings. In those busy years of the late 1940's and early 1950s, Ken Bradshaw and his driver would go with an old 'Lanky A Class' engine and a set of coaches to places like Bolton when it was their holidays, bringing back to Fleetwood a train load of passengers for the Isle of Man. Once unloaded they would back out of the station, run round the stock and go back for another 'mashing'. One winter's day when the wind was biting, Ken had taken a ride on his motor bike into Fleetwood to call at the station and book some steamer tickets at Fred Browns little ticket office. Having got the tickets, he tapped out his pipe and buttoned up his railway overcoat as he walked out of the main entrance. He cranked up the little AJS motorbike and set off along Queen's Terrace, fighting the cold wind. By the time he'd turned into Dock Street, he began to feel quite warm, as smoke began coming out from beneath his overcoat. It was then that he realised his pipe must have still been alight. Quickly stopping, he opened his overcoat to find his inside pocket smouldering and almost about to burst into flame, it was a near thing !

Picture from the archives of
Lighthouse Stationary, North Albert Street, Fleetwood

FLEETWOOD MARKET

Here we are at the market. Visiting Fleetwood's famous Friday market was mum's last treat of the holiday. Going on these Friday outings to Fleetwood appears to have been a long standing tradition in our family. In the war years, mum stayed at Blackpool with relatives and occasionally in guest houses. May be that is when the first outings were made up to Fleetwood. Having walked down Queen's Terrace to the point where the road turned to the right to enter Dock Street, we would then turn into Victoria Street to gain access to the market. Just occasionally, we would leave the station, go straight across the road, up Pharos Street by the Lighthouse, turn left and walk along North Albert Street, which, like Queen's Terrace was and still is an exceptionally wide road. You simply turned left then into Victoria Street.

Pre-war days. The three views on this page all date from before the Second World War. It is thought they may have been taken by the market superintendent of the time. At the top, we see the indoor market. Above we have pre-war 'Chara's' in Dock Street and left we have the outdoor stalls on the Adelaide Street side. The indoor market was quite basic, no frills, simple bare brick walls with a high pitched roof, not unlike a large bus garage in effect. Biscuits, sweets, fudge, and cake stalls, all did well. Farmhouse stalls, selling cheese and home cured meats from farms across the Wyre, were popular. If you needed curtaining, especially net curtains, then this was the place to come. At one time, oil based table cloths were very fashionable, you could have any length or width you wanted. Fleetwood market certainly had a good selection of designs.

The market in later days. As we can see, the market by the 1950's was still a busy affair. Possibly in the region of three to four thousand people in total would arrive by motor coaches and as we have already seen half of those coaches would comfortably be able to park up along Dock Street. Queen's Terrace and certain other wide streets were also used as coach parking areas. A lot of people also came by train and many of those on holiday in Blackpool simply took a tram ride north. This view is looking up Adelaide Street towards Dock Street. The railway runs at right angles to this street and is hidden by the buildings in the distance. The land in the far distance is across the river Wyre at Preesall and Knott end. The large archway over to the left leads into the main hall of the market. Once inside, I seem to recall the market had two very distinct areas that were slightly separated or maybe that is where the market was at sometime extended to meet the demands of the customer. Outside, bounded by Adelaide Street on one side and Victoria Street on the other side, was a mass of open air stalls selling everything imaginable. From table lamps, to tin openers and lingerie to light bulbs. **(left)** The annual carnival used to begin its procession from Adelaide Street, by the market, and here we see part of it heading down Lord Street near St Peter's Church possibly in 1963 or 1964. *Tony Bretherton* took this last picture and all the others on these pages came from the archive of *Lighthouse Stationary, North Albert Street, Fleetwood.*

On the edge of the Wyre. From the air we can see here just what the Luftwaffe would have seen of Fleetwood as they passed over the town on their way to bomb Barrow-in-Furness. Mind you, it was dark when they flew over with their 'droning' Heinkel bombers. There is a lot to look at here. Going clockwise round the picture, we will start in the right hand bottom corner with the North Euston Hotel. From down on the ground, it looked such an impressive structure, so long and tall, we never realised it was really all frontage with little behind it. The small lighthouse on the Esplanade comes next, followed by the life boat house, the Memorial gardens and the private bowling greens. Nearby is the dominant structure of the Pharos lighthouse and bottom left is the Knott End ferry terminal and the railway station with Queen's Terrace running along side. Note the long wide road in the middle of the picture, North Albert Street. Continuing up the left side of the picture we can see the railway hugging the side of the deep water basin all the way round to Wyre Dock. The station there is visible as is the railway running towards Wyre Dock Junction, with the gas works on the far right. If you look at the top of the picture, the original trackbed of the railway can be seen out on the salt marshes, close to where there was a foul smelling bone meal factory. The original route ran in a straight line across to Burn Naze.

*Picture from the archive of **Lighthouse Stationary, North Albert Street, Fleetwood***

The 'Regency' look

With scenic views out across the estuary and over towards the Barrow coastline, the North Euston Hotel was the ideal place to stay if you had 'got enough pennies'. In the golden years of rail travel and steamer trips to the Isle of Man, no doubt the well heeled section of the population would have stayed here to break up the journey and take in the sea air. On our trips to Fleetwood, we rarely walked along the Esplanade. It only seemed to happen in the last years when the novelty of dashing by tram down to the South Shore at Blackpool had become less of a priority and treats like the Pleasure Beach were losing their appeal. By the time we did this though there were no big Isle of Man boats to watch on the evening tide backing up the channel into Fleetwood.

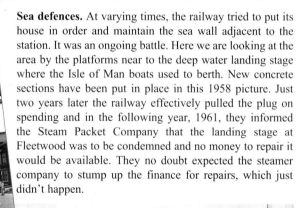

Sea defences. At varying times, the railway tried to put its house in order and maintain the sea wall adjacent to the station. It was an ongoing battle. Here we are looking at the area by the platforms near to the deep water landing stage where the Isle of Man boats used to berth. New concrete sections have been put in place in this 1958 picture. Just two years later the railway effectively pulled the plug on spending and in the following year, 1961, they informed the Steam Packet Company that the landing stage at Fleetwood was to be condemned and no money to repair it would be available. They no doubt expected the steamer company to stump up the finance for repairs, which just didn't happen.

The ferry to Knott End

All three of the ferry boats are just about seen here. The *Lunevale* sets out for Knott End as the *Caldervale* is tied up on the right and just barely visible. Across the water at Knott End is the *Wyresdale* (the one depicted in the postcard). This latter vessel was almost sunk by the suction of the IOM Steam Packet Company's vessel 'King Orry' in June 1955. Just two years later in April 1957, the little ferry's boiler blew up, killing three people.

The Isle of Man Steam Packet Company.

Running between 11 and 18 boats at varying times between the 1920's and the 1960's, the services operated seasonally by the steam packet company between Fleetwood and the Isle of Man were just a portion of the shipping company's activities. Liverpool was the main port of departure for the Isle of Man route. The company also ran services to the island at times from Llandudno, Heysham and Ardrossan, in Scotland. Pleasure cruises were also run from these places on an out and back daily basis in the summer months. Probably all the company's vessels did the Fleetwood run at some time of other. It was however, to be the *Viking* which throughout the years became the most consistent performer in and out of Fleetwood. She is seen above at the No. 1 berth by the station at Fleetwood. Completed on the Tyne in 1905, her maiden voyage was on the 26th of June that year. Forty nine years and two World Wars later, she made her final trip out of Fleetwood for Douglas on 14th August 1954. By the 1950's she'd outlived all other Victorian 'Titanic' looking ships of the big funnel variety. The steam packet company ships played their part in the evacuations from Dunkirk in 1940, Britain's darkest hour. Three of the company's ships were lost there between the 29th and 30th of May. The six year old *Mona's Isle* struck a mine and sank, losing 24 crew members, most of whom were from the Isle of Man. The 1937 built *Fenella* sank upright in the harbour at Dunkirk after a bombing raid and the old *King Orry* of 1913 sank out at sea after being attacked from the air. In all, 24,669 allied personnel were brought home on steam packet company vessels. The company's ships also brought back thousands of troops from Le Havre, Cherbourg and Brest in July 1940, the *Manxman*, cheekily sailing out of Cherbourg harbour as the Germans were coming in. The *Viking* also lifted 1,800 children off the Channel Islands in July of 1940 as the Germans were about to invade. Because of the bombing and mines in the channels out of Liverpool, the steam packet company transferred all its operations and offices from Liverpool to Fleetwood for the duration of the war. When D-day came, three of the company's vessels were commandeered as command ships sitting off shore at Normandy. *Ben-My–Chree* was at Omaha beach, the *Lady of Mann'* was at Juno beach and the *Victoria* was at Arramanches and Utah beachheads. The post war years were brilliant in terms of passenger figures, the years from 1948-53 being exceptional. It was in 1948 that the illuminations went on again in Blackpool for the first time following the darkness of the war years and in September that year the steamer *Snaefell* (No. 5) spent a week on evening trips from Fleetwood sailing down to Blackpool for the 'Lights'.

Regular performers in the company's fleet to work into Fleetwood appear to be the *Viking* and the *Lady of Mann* also fairly regular were *Mona's Isle*, *Fenella*, *Victoria*, *Snaefell*, *Rushen Castle*, *King Orry* and the beautiful old Ben, *Ben-My–Chree* (No.4). In those busy years of the early 1950's, three boats were booked away from Fleetwood a few minutes apart at about 10.30am. There was a 3.30pm afternoon sailing and an early morning one as well. The Isle of Man was in many respects like going abroad and had been treated as such for a great many years. In the later 1950's, holidaymakers found they really could afford to go abroad properly and that the weather was more reliable and the ability to say you had spent your holidays abroad somewhere the majority of us couldn't go, had a definite appeal all of it's own. Douglas as a resort on the Isle of Man tended to be Victorian in its outlook, a bit like Llandudno or Weymouth for example, and where as mainland resorts such as these found the way to change their appeal, Douglas sadly took a lot longer come to terms with the changing needs of the holidaymaker. There never could have been a lasting return to the Isle of Man's popularity of the 1930's. That was a different era, in another life. By the 1960's and 1970's we were truly living in a different age.

Go abroad to the ISLE of MAN!

(above) The 'Lady of Mann', the Isle of Man Steam Packet Company's centenary vessel of 1930, was a regular visitor to Fleetwood. This flagship vessel is seen backing up the Wyre estuary into Fleetwood in the 1930's still wearing her all white livery of 1933. She typifies the modern world just prior to the Second World War. When thinking about those years and of Fleetwood and the Isle of Man, George Formby instantly comes to mind. However comical and silly you may have thought of him, his films of the late 1930's and the 1940's easily outsold the best American films at British box offices. The popularity of the film *No Limit*, a comedy set around the TT races on the Isle of Man and the fact that it was possible to see George both at Fleetwood at times and over in Douglas on the island, gave a certain edge to the era, an aura almost. Things had however changed by the late 1940's, and the motor bikes had become seriously competitive machines, ridden by young men like twenty-two year old John Surtees. In 1956, he won the senior event on his MV Augusta (81), with an average speed for the seven laps of the mountain circuit of 96.57mph.

End of an era

As the 1950's progressed, the Isle of Man's dependable traditional and scenic attributes began to lose their appeal. Going abroad, as the 1960's approached, meant just more than a trip across the Irish Sea. Douglas became expensive and not good value for money. Ideals change and although the passengers still came for the steamers, the figures continued to go down with the passing years. The railway, cash strapped and under serious financial and structural review as the 1960's dawned, realised it could no longer afford any operations of just a seasonal nature. The summer only excursions and anything connected with this would have to be phased out. The landing stage at Fleetwood, an ageing timber construction, was due for some serious repairs. A figure of £750,000 had been mentioned as being needed. It was clear the railway was not going to do the repairs and in view of the steadily falling numbers travelling on the steam packet company boats, they too didn't want to fund repairs. The announcement soon came in 1961 that the Isle of Man boats would cease operations from Fleetwood with effect from the 11th of September. It fell to *Mona's Queen*, seen above at the South Edward pier at Douglas to perform that final sailing. Leaving Fleetwood at 10.30am she had on board 1,193 passengers for the crossing. The following week she went into mothballs and in November the following year (1962), she sailed off to become a Greek cruise ship called the *Fiesta*. The last inward sailing to Fleetwood brought *Mona's Isle* and after off-loading, she too went into store at Barrow. Appropriately, when sailings were restored seasonally ten years later on 25th August 1971, it fell to *Mona's Isle* to work the first sailing out of Fleetwood.

FLEETWOOD

SCENES FROM THE PAST : 26 - PART SIX
JOURNEYS BY EXCURSION TRAIN FROM EAST LANCASHIRE
A REPRISE - FEATURING

SOUTHPORT, MORECAMBE AND BLACKPOOL

THE FINAL CHAPTER

BLACKPOOL NORTH

THE END OF STEAM 1964 - 1967

Foxline   STUART TAYLOR

'All Squared-up'

It is farewell to Fleetwood, as driver Jim Hornby opens 48756 up for the dash to the shed at the end of another shift. This is where we should have come to the end of our excursion story............but there's more. Well just one more book, a final round up of the end of the excursion era full of exceptional pictures taken at Blackpool North in the years of 1965 to 1967. Truly atmospheric scenes that capture the middle 1960s perfectly and deeply contrast with the pictures seen in the earlier volumes. This final book now in preparation is in fact two volumes in one. The first half of the book covers in reprise form the story of the five previous volumes and overlooks the story using many unseen pictures. It is a fitting end to a well liked series.